T0364948

Uncluttered Management Thinking

Prof. Dr. oec. habil. Fredmund Malik is widely known for his clear and precise language. As scientist, author, consultant, and management trainer he has provided guidance for executives of all levels, organizations, and industries for more than 30 years. Based in St. Gallen, Switzerland, Professor Malik is also an entrepreneur and the owner of Malik Management, with approximately 250 employees in St. Gallen, Zurich, Vienna, Berlin, London, Shanghai, and Toronto. His latest English book published by Campus is *Management. The Essence of the Craft.*

Fredmund Malik

Uncluttered Management Thinking

46 Concepts for Masterful Management

Translated from German by Jutta Scherer,
JS textworks (Munich, Germany)

Campus Verlag
Frankfurt / New York

Bibliographic information published by Deutsche Nationalbibliothek:
The Deutsche Nationalbibliothek lists this publication in the Deutsche National-bibliografie. Detailed bibliographic data is available in the internet at http://dnb.d-nb.de
ISBN 978-3-593-39365-0

Cover design: Hißmann, Heilmann, Hamburg
Typesetting: Publikations Atelier, Dreieich
Printing: Druckhaus „Thomas Müntzer", Bad Langensalza
Printed in Germany

www.campus.de

Content

Foreword 7

Psychological Errors 13

Charisma 15
Enthusiasm 18
Job Hopper 21
Talent 25
Potential 27
Making Mistakes 29
Challenge 32
Trust 37
Motivation 41
Praise 43
Performance Limits 45
Burnout and Stress 49
Identification 52
Risk Appetite 57
Fun 61

Management Errors 65

Management Style 67
Leadership 72
Images of Man 76

Staffing Decisions 80
Teamwork 83
Vision 88
Emotion 92
Focus 98
Managerial Compensation 101
Knowledge Management 104
Top Management Teams 109
Coaching 113
Innovation 116
Culture 120
Customer 126
Growth 129

Economic Errors 133

Shareholder 135
Stakeholder 138
Inflation and Deflation 143
U.S. Management Superiority 146
EBIT, EBITDA 149
Stock Options 151
U.S. Economic Miracle 154
Corporate Success 157
Value 161
Sustainability 164
Globalization 166
Profit 170
Interest Rate Cuts 172
Doing Business 174
Rationality 178

Notes 181
References 183

Foreword

An IT specialist will do anything to keep his hard disk clear of viruses. Everyone knows how dangerous they are. But how to prevent mental "viruses" – dangerous ideas – from getting into people's heads? That is at least as important as virus protection for computers: wrong concepts, theories, and ideas are the root causes of wrong management, and the words used in an organization play a crucial part.

The recent economic misdevelopments and excesses were largely due to a general confusion of speech and thinking. It is not some kind of hindsight know-it-all attitude that makes me adopt this critical position; rather, I have been advocating and publicizing this view since the early 1990s.

Without the confusion of language there would have been no such nonsense as the New Economy, which was supposed to arise from what was naïvely described as the miracles of informatization and digitalization (without any material value being added); nor would we have been haunted by the specter of shareholder value, which resulted in one of the gravest misallocations ever of economic resources. There would have been none of the outrageous balance-sheet tampering, nor would a wave of start-ups and IPOs have been confused with real innovation. How such a thing as "cash burn rate" could ever become a respected term in the evaluation of companies is beyond me. It is a question that ought to be answered by mass psychologists, in particular those specializing in stock market hysteria. Without all that language confusion, the mirage of the U.S. economy's worldwide superiority – which was eagerly and uncritically disseminated by the media – would have been an outright impossibility. Last but not least, the global financial and economic crisis we are in has resulted from psychological and management errors.

Clear language, an instrument of clear thinking, would have created the differentiation and skepticism that are indispensable for aligning both the business world and society as a whole with reality.

What George Orwell could only sketch out roughly in *1984* has been carried to the extreme in neoliberal media society, during the decade that marked the transition into the third millennium. The result is a serious, perhaps tenacious "virus infection" of one of society's most important organs: management. And even if that disease is cured some day, when a new generation of managers will have come of age, it will take many years until the harm it has done will be remedied and its effects will be overcome.

Clear Language as a Basis for Good Management

Anyone wishing to manage a company or any other institution correctly and effectively ought to pay special attention to the issue of language. Some terms are best avoided entirely; for others, their proper use should be clearly specified. How far this should be taken depends on the individual case. Some people may have good reasons to keep using certain "dangerous" words, despite all reservations. They should, however, always be aware of the risks associated with those words – risks of misunderstandings and, more importantly, of wrong decisions.

For instance, the CEO of a leading bank had the courage to ban foreign words. That may be taking it a bit too far, but it is a brave move and helps enhance clarity, comprehensibility, and successful communication. What is more, it is an effective guard against bluffers and boasters. Such a ban does not represent an infringement of basic rights, such as the right to freedom of expression: any member of staff can and should express his opinions freely, of course – all that is required of him is that he do so using intelligible language.

In this book, I will deal with a series of words the use of which, in my view, is a bad habit and in some cases even dangerously misleading – such as "vision" and "leadership". Some of them are terms for which a misguided usage has developed over time (e.g., "staffing decisions") or an entirely wrong concept has emerged ("U.S. management superiority"). They are all words that have been used so often in recent years that they have become standard terms of management and their meanings have turned into widespread (and erroneous) beliefs.

In some cases, the words in question are the manifestation and result of temporary fashions. Management in general is strongly infiltrated by fads, more than any other field. As long as something is in fashion, it is usually asserted dogmatically and even with inquisitorial zeal, in particular by those who shape those fashions – often consulting firms for which they constitute the foundation of their business. However, quite a lot of the words discussed here also result from poor management training, in that people fail to recognize fashions for what they are.

Many managers have never had the opportunity to acquire sound expertise in corporate management. All they have is rather superficial knowledge, which, as we know, is often more dangerous than having no knowledge at all.

It is a clear sign of good management if counter-measures are taken against such developments. Achieving effective communication and real understanding in an organization is difficult enough as it is, one reason being the rather limited linguistic skills most managers have. If matters are made even worse by the use of wrong and misleading terms, good communication almost impossible.

The danger of the terms discussed here lies not only in this general difficulty of communication; what is even worse is that they cause errors, thus misguiding the thoughts and actions of managers and employees. They convey concepts of how to manage companies, how to deal with employees, and how to treat customers, which are detrimental to companies' interests and sometimes even cause their demise.

The terms I rate as "dangerously misleading" serve many purposes. They are used to shape opinions, policies, and businesses, to pursue interests and to legitimize status. They are also used in an attempt to impress others.

Impressing others is the strategy of a certain type of intellectual and expert. Making an impression is the most important basis of their existence; indeed, it is the only one. They will therefore do anything to maintain semantic appearances – as pseudo-scientists, as éminences grises in their organizations, in staff functions and committees, as consultants, experts, therapists, and gurus. Their preferred tools are clouds of language, pompous terms and fancy catchwords.

Good managers do not let themselves be impressed, at least not permanently.

More Than Just Linguistic Subtleties

I am not talking about linguistic subtleties here or about matters of style or taste, but about the right way of thinking and about effective communication. These "dangerous" words are a source of misunderstandings. They hamper effective communication and give rise to misguided expectations, and as a result, they cause employees to act the wrong way. In extreme cases they even make an organization unmanageable.

What is at stake here is clarity, comprehensibility, and professional precision. Clear and accurate terminology is one of the hallmarks of a highly developed science or discipline. Mastery of its terms is an indispensable ingredient to professionalism and competence.

For instance, no one would be taken seriously in engineering or natural sciences if he did not know how to distinguish velocity from acceleration. A lawyer unable to tell the difference between ownership and possession, or between renting and leasing, would not only be considered incompetent but even a danger to potential clients. He could not be entrusted with a property law case. When it comes to fine but significant distinctions, clarity and precision are all the more important.

Much the same happens in management, not as an exception but regularly. We are far from having achieved the accuracy that has long become natural in other disciplines. In almost every discussion with managers I cannot help but realize that, as professional as they may be in their respective fields, they lack clear positions in management terminology.

Mere definitions and etymological clarifications are not what I have in mind. Each of the words discussed in this book represents a wrong theory, a widespread and influential yet misleading management concept. My chief concern is to put them right, thus providing a basis for better and more responsible management.

Psychological Errors

Charisma

We need charismatic leaders! is a demand which has been made for some time now, and with increasing urgency.

Unquestionably, it is not enough for managers to be able to read and write and be human beings of average decency. They have higher requirements to meet. But does that warrant going to the other extreme? Somehow the idea has sprung up that a manager, in particular one at the top, ought to be a mixture of Albert Einstein, Alexander the Great and Bob Hope – a universal genius ... a one-man band of business.

People have learnt to put up with a great deal of nonsense on the subject of management. Now charisma, on top of everything else? That makes the nonsense dangerous. After all the experiences of the past century, should we not be a little more cautious and, perhaps, think before we speak? Was not the 20th century the epoch of charismatic leaders? Do the names Hitler, Stalin, and Mao Tse Tung ring a bell?

Significantly, it is always the English word "leader" that we use in German-speaking regions. No one dares call the thing by its German name: *Führer*. In some cases it may be better, due to translation issues, to stick with the English term – but for "leader" there is a very simple, accurate and crystal-clear German translation. However, it is a term that may get in the way of fantasizing and romanticizing about charisma. A brief glance at the dictionary or at Max Weber's sociological work would also help avoid the worst of the nonsense.[2]

In our much-invoked knowledge society, real knowledge seems to be the commodity least in demand when it comes to the subject of management.

Historically, charismatic leaders have almost always produced catastrophes – in every field. True leaders do not need charisma. They lead by self-discipline and example, not by grand slogans and shouts of hooray. Their capital is not charisma but trust.

I am not denying that charisma has an effect on people. That, however, is the very reason why the crucial point is not *whether* we are led but to *where*. The effect that leaders have is important but it has to be controlled by responsibility and by the kind of goals that are set.

Charismatic leaders are dangerous because they do not stick to the rules. They are unpredictable, they consider themselves the masters of the universe, they pursue utopian ideas. They are convinced they are right in everything they do, they become inflexible, and this is precisely why they soon come to follow the wrong course. They are not leaders but misleaders. A theory of leadership that has no place for this distinction is worthless.

Some highly effective leaders of the 20th century had no charisma at all, among them Dwight D. Eisenhower, George C. Marshall, and Harry Truman in America or Konrad Adenauer and Kurt Schumacher in Germany. And in the 19th century there was hardly anyone with less charisma than Florence Nightingale, Abraham Lincoln, or Henry Dunant. All these people are prime candidates for the accolade of true leadership, though in very different fields.

Charisma – and this is something that can easily be demonstrated – is neither necessary nor desirable for true leadership or right management. Of course, it cannot be ruled out that charismatic personalities may occasionally be good leaders or managers *as well* but, because of their effect on people, they are always exposed to major hazards and great temptations. And they are always a risk.

It may be true that, as is so often claimed, the 21st century needs leaders. However, after the disasters of the 20th century it would be advisable not to tolerate a concept of leadership that is so blind to history.

Enthusiasm

A leader must be able enthuse people.

That, or something to the effect, is what magazines and books are full of; it is a popular opinion and something that comes up in virtually every discussion. Statements of this kind are standard features in the tools applied by headhunters and assessment specialists – selection and evaluation processes, as well as the expert opinions based on them – and they are standard criteria in competence tests.

People assume a positive relationship between enthusiasm and performance: the more enthusiastic someone is about a given task, or so the argument goes, the better he will perform. It certainly seems perfectly plausible – but where is the proof?

There is none. Apparently nobody has noticed so far: there is not a single study that has even brought up the issue, let alone provided evidence of that relationship.

Possible studies would fail due to the simple fact that enthusiasm can be neither measured nor operationalized, nor can enthusiasm be created for the purposes of an experiment. It is true that the proposition about enthusiasm sounds "somehow" convincing, but as a matter of fact it is sheer superstition. There are two opposing propositions I would like to make:

1. The more enthusiastic someone is about something, the less he typically knows about the subject and the more questionable are therefore his abilities and performance.
2. Real performance – and in particular peak performance – does not require any enthusiasm; on the contrary: enthusiasm tends to be a hindrance. What is needed are expertise and experience.

These two propositions may sound rather daring at first, but there is plenty of evidence to support them. We all know people who ski or play tennis with great enthusiasm, albeit very poorly. And most of us know others who master those sports to perfection – but they do so with little enthusiasm. They may enjoy their sports, but usually only as long as they pursue them as a hobby. Anyone who has made a profession of them – say, as a skiing instructor or a tennis pro – is driven much more by a sense of duty and professionalism, perhaps also by the need to meet contractual obligations, by ambition, or by greed, than by enthusiasm. Even the most exciting occupation cannot evoke enough enthusiasm to last a lifetime. No one can be enthusiastic permanently; enthusiasm fades over time. It is not something that craftsmen, laborers, teachers, waiters, nurses, doctors, or managers in business need to do their jobs – nor is it of any use to them.

If you look for peak performance, consider sports, in particular pro sports and the challenges associated with it. Before a difficult competition, an experienced athlete will be anything but enthusiastic; he or she would not even know how enthusiasm could be helpful.

What does help is the certainty to have trained adequately, to master the discipline, to be in peak form. I have experienced this myself innumerable times in mountaineering, and all the trip reports ever written about difficult to extreme ascents only prove my point. Only for easy ascents is there such a thing as enthusiasm. And even if there is some enthusiasm when preparing for or starting an expedition, it never lasts long enough to get anyone to the summit. Different things are needed for that. There may be enthusiasm once the summit has been reached, but the performance has already been delivered then. Also, enthusiasm will only materialize if the climbers are not faced with a long and difficult descent, as in that case they will need to deliver even more performance – quite frequently of the more difficult kind. No, enthusiasm is not a category preceding or enabling performance. Enthusiasm comes *afterwards*.

Job Hopper

During the boom years, people were virtually taught and led to bluff – in fact, even forced to. All that prattle about ego marketing, the "war for talent", the recruiting events at certain firms, the fashion of self-publicizing – all these things in combination more or less forced those not normally inclined towards such behavior to play along.

It usually becomes obvious at a young age who tends to rely on bluff and appearances, and who aims for substantial values and true performance. Clearly more than half of my students and our younger training attendants – both within and outside our firm – were and are disgusted with having to grandstand in order to get anywhere. They even perceive it to be a form of prostitution. This nonsense has created a stage for the wrong people – the "lightest-weight" experts – and has won them the attention of a certain kind of media.

One of the most important and also most difficult tasks in a company, no matter what its size, is selecting the right people for vacant positions. How to separate the wheat from the chaff, the bluffers from the true performers?

These days it is more critical than ever to know what to look for.

Positions or Achievements

In business and politics alike, a certain type of manager has often ascended to senior and top positions. This type is extraordinarily skillful in concealing his true incompetence; he masters rituals and small talk; he knows whom and how to flatter; he manages to get the ear of those who matter.

Today's society – or rather, widespread errors in staffing decisions – often make it easy for him to gain influence, as people will pay attention to positions rather than achievements

I want to call particular attention to this type of manager. We encounter him quite often, as a result of misguided staffing policies and misunderstood concepts of career-making: It is the job hopper.

Job hoppers are people who collect positions – transitory positions – rather than achievements. Their CVs are highly impressive at first glance: they contain lengthy lists of previously held positions, often with important-looking titles like "Executive Assistant", "Coordinator", "Representative of", "Member of", or "Contributor to". To European ears, all those titles sound particularly impressive in English. If someone's business card says "Chief Group Coordinator", no one will dare ask that person what he actually does for a living.

At closer analysis, there are two things you will not usually find in a CV: the person's responsibility and achievements – specifically, his being held responsible for what he has achieved (or failed to achieve). That, however, is the only thing that really matters in business.

More often than not, people with long lists of positions are not effective managers but careerists. In their resumés you will find plenty of things, in their life only one: an unerring instinct for when they had better move on. And they invariably choose to leave just a few months before their lack of achievements – or, in some cases, the mess they are going to leave behind – starts to show.

Job Rotation

In many large corporations, the disregard of people's achievements is actively promoted: through poorly understood job rotation.

Its purpose, of course, is a perfectly correct one: to ensure a maximum of practical training and experience for promising employees. There is nothing to be said against the principle as such – only it needs to be applied correctly. Job rotation can only unfold its positive effects if tangible results are achieved at each station.

The fact that there is such a thing as an excessive amount of time spent in one position is generally accepted. The opposite seems less clear: an increasing number of executives – in particular the younger ones – hold their positions for much too short a time to achieve results. They often rotate on to the next job before the work is done and results materialize.

Job rotation is good and important for people in their twenties, and it is needed again for those reaching forty-plus. The critical age group, however, are those between thirty and forty. These people must be given an opportunity to achieve what is most important in life – the very source of confidence, self-assuredness, self-respect, lifelong self-motivation, and, above all, credibility and natural authority. These spring from one thing alone: visible, convincing results. Not from positions.

There are no absolute numbers for the optimal tenure in a position, and thus for job hopping – but there is a straightforward criterion: A person needs to stay in a position long enough to achieve results that are visible and convincing to others. I am not denying that this can sometimes be done in a year and a half or two, but there are not very many serious tasks for which tangible results – results that truly matter – can be achieved within 24 months. Viewed realistically, it will take longer in most cases.

Anyone who has held more than three or four positions between the ages of thirty and forty will have to be prepared to answer a few questions. And he will be well-advised to think carefully about the answers, in particular when talking to a capable personnel manager.

That manager will ask him things like: What did you do before? What were your main achievements? What was this position like when you obtained it and what did it look like when you left? What are you particularly proud of? Why?

A job hopper will not really have good answers. In all likelihood, he will be trying to gloss over his lack of skill – thereby bringing onto himself the pressures of a lifelong lie: having to pretend something he will never be able to prove for the rest of his work life.

Talent

One of the greatest deceptions of the past years in human resources management was triggered by the grand phrase "war for talent". The martial term "war" alone should be enough to raise suspicios. But if we do want to talk about "war", it is much more a "war for performance".

There is hardly a presentation by HR people these days that does not contain the word "talent". When asked what exactly they mean by it, most of them begin to hew and haw, finally coming up with a vague answer along the lines of: "…someone with special skills… someone capable …"

I suggest largely dispensing with the word "talent": it is just another term that directs attention to the unusual, the rare, the special – as is so often the case in our current understanding of management. It is not without reason that e.g. the Merriam Webster online dictionary defines talent (among other things) as *"the natural endowments of a person; a special, often athletic, creative, or artistic aptitude; a person of talent or a group of persons of talent in a field or activity"*. Nowadays it is, without doubt, used more generally to refer to skilled, capable workers, but it should be considered a misleading term due to its connotation of "rare capabilities" that most of these people do not possess.

I do not deny that there is such a thing as talent. What I deny is that it is of major significance for the success of a company. It is not talent that is needed in management but results. Everyone knows plenty of people who can certainly be considered talented but who have never achieved anything. The opposite is equally well known: people who have hardly any talent worth mentioning, yet who perform and achieve amazing results. However, if people feel they cannot do without the word "talent" entirely, they should at least confine it to the *use* of one's talent. After all, talent itself is not important but what we make of it.

I would also advise against talking about "capable people". Nobody is just "capable" – the question is always: capable *of what*?

What we need is clarity about the specific strengths a person has. Strengths are not the same as talents. They are much more mundane, much more definite, and much more practical. In discussions I have on the subject, people using the word "talent" often do a sudden about-face, claiming to mean the same by "talent" as I do by strength. This is similar to the confusion mentioned above between ownership and possession, or renting and leasing. It is juggling with terms and using bogus labels, and it takes the place of clarity and precision.

Potential

"Potential" is a word that falls into the same category as "talent", and is often used synonymously with it. This is true especially for its popular emphatic form, "high potentials", meaning "promising people". My suggestion is to pay attention not to potential but to performance, and to speak of "high performance" rather than "high potential".

The two things are not the same. Potential is a possibility, a promise (quite commonly an empty one, as it often turns out), something one can base one's hopes on. Performance is something that has been demonstrated before, something one can truly build on.

It is downright impossible to reliably assess potential. The only things that can be accurately determined are the performance that someone has shown in the past and the strengths he or she has demonstrated in so doing. Everything else is surmise, hope, and projection.

There is no practicable method of detecting potential as such. All we can ever do is infer future achievements from previous ones. Attention therefore needs to be focused on performance shown in the past, not on some nebulous potential. When positions have to be filled, what is needed is a list of performers from which to choose, rather than a list of potentials.

Decision-makers in well-managed firms do not rely on potentials. The word as such can be used but it is important to pay close attention to what is meant by it. The only foundation for the assessments of potential is tests of actual performance as well as practical probationary tests.

There is yet another thing that is essential, even crucial: Both terms – talent and potential – imply that attention is only directed to the person, as if all prerequisites for success were to be found there. This, however, overlooks the fact that impact and success depend on two elements: the person with his or her specific strengths, and the particular task to be carried out. Note that I am not talking about the "function" or "position" but about the "task" to be performed, or, even more precisely, about the person's *assignment*. That is something entirely different from the position; it is the key priority determining, for the immediate foreseeable future, what is do be done in that position.

Anyone who wishes to get people to perform and who needs results for the company will have to match people's strengths with the assignments at hand. Admittedly, that is not easy. But it is certainly easier to change assignments than people. Due to the fixation on people, the second element, the assignment, is almost always forgotten. Well-managed companies put major emphasis on assignments. That is how they achieve break-through successes – and they do it with perfectly ordinary people, because not even they have universal geniuses on their payrolls.

Making Mistakes

Is it alright to make mistakes? Time and again, managers – including those in senior positions – announce with visible pride that in their organizations people are permitted to make mistakes. They do so in the obvious conviction that this is evidence of their being particularly advanced.

I used to have intense discussions on the subject. These days, all I do is ask a couple of questions: Would you get on an aircraft if you knew that the airline was proud of the fact its pilots are allowed to make mistakes? Would you take your wife, your children or your parents to a hospital whose code of practice said that mistakes are permitted? And would you buy medication from a pharmaceutical company that insisted that its staff could make mistakes?

Of course, the answer always is, "Ah, but that was not what I meant..." Well, what did you mean? It is remarkable how much nonsense has crept into management theory and how uncritical even seasoned managers can be – individuals, after all, to whom economic resources and the fate of people are entrusted.

Many feel they are showing great wisdom if they make a distinction: it is permitted to make mistakes, but never the same mistake twice. Admittedly, that is a bit better – but still not good enough. There are mistakes that must not be made at all, not even once. How often can a pharmacist be allowed to dispense the wrong medication?

Next, my discussion partner will usually try another variation: mistakes are permitted, but it is essential to learn from them. That, too, cannot be allowed to stand. If a patient dies because his nurse used the wrong syringe, it is not much use to him if she learns from her mistake.

Mistakes happen, even with the best of management. That is a fact we have to live with. But to turn that into a license for making mistakes, to be proud of it and promote it as a particular advance in management – that is dangerous.

The maxim that needs to be applied in management is: mistakes must not be made. That is the basic principle that should guide all actions.

Only when this principle has been accepted is it permissible to make meaningful distinctions: for example, a certain degree of experimentation must be possible in a company and in the process there will be mistakes. That, however, is very different from "being allowed to make mistakes" in the sense outlined above. Experiments are done under controlled conditions and in such a way that mistakes cannot have any serious consequences. Another case where mistakes clearly have to be tolerated is where people are trained and instructed, but that, too, is something that is almost always kept separate from everyday business, under supervision and direction, until one can be reasonably sure that no further mistakes will be made. That is the very purpose of training.

A frequent objection against the view presented here is that there are organizations where people no longer do anything at all, simply for fear of making mistakes. That is true; such organizations exist. In my practice as a consultant I have repeatedly come across them. It goes without saying that these organizations are sick.

A number of factors may be responsible for this, foremost among them serious errors of management in dealing with the very question of mistakes. Nevertheless, the solution cannot be to suddenly start preaching that mistakes are permissible.

For all the jobs and professions in a modern-day society, the rule is that mistakes must not happen. This rule applies to heart surgeons, auditors and pilots. Why should managers be an exception? Only a certain kind of allegedly avant-garde, but in fact downright stupid management gurus seem to believe that it does not apply to them – that they can afford to simply carry on with the carelessness of their early-childhood sandpit days. They seem to live in a world where such things as professionalism or the duty of care do not exist. Apparently they have never heard of liability or damages. And, lamentably, there are executives who lack either the brains or the courage to put a stop to such people's doings. Or, even worse, they imitate the nonsense they propagate and introduce it in their companies.

Mistakes must not happen – that has to be the ground rule. From there, we may start relaxing the principle very selectively: when, where and by whom and under what circumstances may mistakes be made and what are the mistakes that must not happen at all? Anything else means replacing responsible management with fads and simple-minded beliefs.

Challenge

Ever since the onset of the latest recession, the average person has probably understood that commercial enterprises are not shelters for those in search of happiness, well-being, or self-fulfillment. They cannot be. Clear-sighted people have always pointed this out, even though – depending on what the zeitgeist called for – they were often despised for it.

Still, it is astonishing how the craze (or craziness) for self-fulfillment keeps popping up again and again – especially (and especially well-masked) where one would least expect it: not in the average employee but in a certain kind of „managerlings" who think of themselves as particularly performance-oriented and dynamic. There is a sure proof way of recognizing them: they love talking about challenges, and how they need a new one over and over again.

Egomania

Many people seem to think that the search for challenges is a clear, strong and positive sign of aptitude. In fact, it is a proof of incompetence. Candidates applying for a job frequently emphasize their interest in the "new challenge" it represents, and many a manager changing into a new position has pointed out the challenges awaiting him when asked about the reasons.

In some cases this may be nothing but idle talk: it is bad enough if it happens in front of the cameras, and unacceptable with managers who should be expected, more than anyone else, to think before they talk. Often these people are not good managers but simply egocentrics – some even full-blown egomaniacs – on their journey to self-fulfillment, usually in combination with a penchant for visions. That makes them an outright danger.

Their concern is not what the company needs but what they themselves need. Their reference point is their want rather than their duty. They do not really care whether they are able to cope with the challenges they so desperately crave – never mind whether they will ever achieve any results.

With that special mixture of naïveté and arrogance they usually have, but entirely in harmony with the zeitgeist, they feel up to anything as long as it "challenges" them – as if an inner feeling of challenge was evidence of their aptitude. They need the "kick"; preferably one that will also make headlines. Coupled with the visions these people often suffer from, this means that their successors are left (usually after a relatively short period of time) with half-finished tasks, sometimes a shambles – while they themselves are moving on to pastures new, to yet another challenge. Shining examples have been found even at noble addresses in the world of finance, the international telecommunication scene and, of course, at the New Economy playground.

I remember a top manager who, in the context of a surprisingly swift job change, informed an astounded public via several TV interviews and talkshows that he regularly needed a new challenge. Worse even, he literally said that if he did not get sweaty palms he saw no fun in a job and had to go looking for another. It was painfully obvious how impressed some of the commentators were, how much they loved his grand phrases, how they believed him to be the epitome of modern management – and how they failed to realize that they were only giving him a platform for spouting embarrasingly juvenile, and for glossing over a veritable disaster.

Overstrain

Could it possibly be that sweaty palms are a sign not of outstanding skill but of the exact opposite – of hopeless overstrain? What would we think of a pilot who got sweaty palms when faced with the challenge of an intercontinental flight? Or of a surgeon who started perspiring because he felt the upcoming operation to be a major challenge? Would we not recommend them to keep practicing until they could perform their tasks in a calm and composed manner, without any adrenaline surges or overreacting perspiratory glands – or, in other words: professionally?

"Going beyond the limits", as is often heard, can be perfectly alright – but only for people capable of recognizing their limits. People who will then think about how they might possibly exceed those limits, with the necessary degree of prudence and based on a clear understanding of the risks involved. Many people, even some of the best in their fields, have failed nonetheless. Reinhold Messner who, like few others, has regularly exceeded limits in alpinism, is one of the first to teach us how to avoid fatal risks rather than seek them, and how to stay "within limits". His true strength is not heroism but cool calculation and professional preparation.

Adventure or Achievement?

It has become fashionable these days to use impressive images of extreme situations in mountaineering for the purpose of advertising and self-portrayal. Quite revealingly, these themes are particularly popular amongst accounting firms, consultancies, investment bankers, and New Economy enterprises – in short, where the ruins from the Bubble Economy pile up highest.

Extreme rock-climbing, frozen waterfalls, high-alpinism – themes like these are a perfect means to attract attention because they symbolize "going beyond the limits". Since I have been practicing alpinism all my life, and at elevated degrees of difficulty, I have looked into the question more closely – and I have not found a single manager at one of those organizations who was even close to measuring up to the subjects of such self-publicizing advertisement. The climbing of Mount Chimborazo is one of the things that some managers (or management consultants) particularly like to boast about – incidentally, always in the presence of yellow-press photographers and in places which can certainly be reached by car. That is truly "beyond the limits" – the limits of embarrassment, not those of performance.

There are managers who are excellent sportsmen, even practising extreme sports – open-sea sailing, extreme and high alpinism, polar and desert expeditions – but you will hardly find them at those firms that attempt to impress the public with such spectacular themes.

Of course it is alright to feel challenged at times, as long as the sensation does not conceal what is actually a lack of professional competence. And while I am all for exploring and exceeding one's performance limits, I recommend skepticism and scrutiny when managers put particular emphasis on the challenges they supposedly need and seek. Also, I have no objections to challenges that are met and adventures that are sought: in private, at extreme sports, on the racing track, in the bivouac.

Companies, however, do not need adventures. They need achievements. Their purpose is not to give their managers adrenaline boosts and sweaty palms. Their purpose is to transform the strengths of their staff into value for their customers.

Trust

While the word "trust" in itself is not dangerous, there are two dangers associated with it: the first is that the significance of trust is overlooked because everyone is fixated on motivation; the second is the danger of turning trust into an emotional problem.

As I have repeatedly said, management training today is dominated by a limited number of topics, including motivation and leadership style. As a result, the importance of trust is disregarded.

This becomes obvious as soon as we take a closer look at a frequent phenomenon that appears paradoxical: There are managers who, although they do everything wrong – at least by textbook standards – have an excellent situation in their company or area of responsibility, including a good working climate and strong performance orientation among their people. Then there are those who do everything correctly according to current management theory and training, who are familiar with recommendations on leadership style as well as with motivation theories and who duly observe them, yet achieve the exact opposite: a bad working climate in their organizations, frustrated employees, and a performance-averse corporate culture. Why is that so?

Closer inspection nearly always reveals that neither motivation nor leadership style nor emotional intelligence is key, but that it hinges on whether people trust their superiors. If an executive has managed to gain and keep the trust of those around him – his staff, colleagues, and superiors – then everything else is of minor importance. He has then created what we might call a robust management situation – robust to all the managerial, behavioral, and motivational mistakes that happen every day.

Not that these can be excused or even justified; but they happen even to the best managers, unintentionally and sometimes unnoticed. Managers are not as sensitive as psychologists would like them to be.

So the question is not whether managerial mistakes happen or not, but how serious they are. Organizations must be quite "thick-skinned" in order to be able to function. In companies, particularly in well-managed ones, people are not overly touchy. There is little time, and usually little understanding for oversensitivities. If everything that happens is permanently analyzed and every word that is said – or left unsaid – is weighed, then a company ceases to be an economic institution. It becomes a psychiatric one.

Nothing can be accomplished in an organization without even a minimum of mutual trust. The logic of the situation is both simple and compelling: if and as long as there is trust, there is no need to worry about motivation, working climate, or corporate culture too much. Mind you, I do not want to discourage anyone from dealing with those things. What is much more important, though, is that if there is a lack of trust, all relevant measures will remain ineffectual – or, even worse, counter-productive. Employee motivation efforts and corporate culture programs will often be perceived as particularly sophisticated forms of manipulation, and ultimately sheer cynicism.

In the light of the significance of trust, it is all the more remarkable that while there are hundreds of analyses, papers and books on motivation and leadership style there is precious little about trust. The subject has simply been overlooked by scientists, and for decades practitioners have tolerated wrong doctrines – which are easily recognizable as such – being disseminated in management training.

Trust is the base of any reasonable, humane and, above all, effective form of management. It does not require any special skills or talents, let alone sophisticated theories as are currently being resorted to for all sorts of things.

With regard to the second danger, consider that contrary to popular opinion, trust and distrust are not emotional phenomena, although certain emotional states may be linked to either. Also, it is entirely unnecessary to speak of a "culture of trust" as it often unthinkingly happens.

When I included the subject in my training seminars in the mid-1980s, there was no relevant management literature, apart from a study by Dale Zand.

Trust is not based on certain emotional states. It is a consequence of consistent behavior, reliability, and perhaps what is commonly referred to as personal integrity. A big word indeed, but what it ultimately says is something simple, and something any manager is able to do: Meaning what you say, walking the talk, and sticking to your promises.

Two widespread misunderstandings need to be prevented in this context: Note that "meaning what you say" does not imply saying everything you mean. In the reality of our organizations that would be downright naïve. As a manager, you will always have to think carefully about what you are going to say, to whom, and when. But once you decide to say something you have to really mean it. Secondly, note that the above does not imply that you cannot change your opinion after having expressed it. You can, and it will even be necessary more often in the future, because every organization's situation changes at a faster pace today than perhaps ever before. All you have to do is say very clearly that you changed your opinion, and if you want to be a good manager you will give your reasons.

All of the above does not imply that trust is to replace motivation, or that it is the same as motivation. It is quite different: Of course, it is all the better if trust is accompanied by motivation. In most cases, it will be no problem under these circumstances to motivate people.

The true significance of my above observation is revealed in the negative case, when trust is lacking. Under such circumstances it is useless to try to motivate people. All attempts will remain without effect if there is not even a minimum of trust and, as mentioned before, they will often turn into the very opposite.

Trust does not replace motivation. Trust is a catalyst. Motivation can only take its effect if there is trust. For precisely this reason, so many well-intended and competently designed motivation programs turn out to be ineffective, or even detrimental, much to the surprise of those who initiated them. Motivation programs are usually started when the management of a company deems them necessary due to deteriorating performance, or in an attempt to motivate people to deliver even better performance.

Motivation

Motivation has been the central theme of management training over the past 40 to 50 years. When asked what they consider their most important task, managers will reply immediately and without hesitation: motivating their staff. No other subject has received as much attention in the social sciences; none has been analyzed so often.

That considered, practitioners actually know surprisingly little. Any attempts to sound them out will usually reveal fragmentary knowledge at best. They do not have a clear idea of what the term motivation really means; very few are familiar with the different theories that exist. Only a minority knows what actually needs to be done in order to motivate people.

My suggestion therefore is to go beyond the usual concepts of motivation. More specifically, I suggest abandoning the notion that there will always be someone – a third party, a superior, or some other person – to be motivated by.

Even if you want to accept this notion as useful for ordinary people, it is certainly not feasible for managers. Anyone who wishes to be a manager, or who even dreams of becoming a "leader" some day, will need to go one step further – from motivation to self-motivation. If you wait to be motivated by others you will never get anywhere. You will remain dependent, someone being guided, for the rest of your life. You are a servant to others at heart, even if happenstance, coincidence, or wrong staffing decisions help you ascend to senior-level positions.

Anyone waiting to be motivated by others will keep getting disappointed, for there will not always be someone to motivate him. Hence my advice, which strongly contradicts conventional thinking: Make yourself inwardly independent of motivation by others – learn to motivate yourself. People are much stronger and more autonomous than widespread pseudo-psychological theories can and will admit.

Praise

Praise is one of the strongest motivators. This is widely accepted and needs no further explanation. And it is exactly where the danger of misuse lies. Praise only motivates people if it has any weight, and if it comes from someone they respect.

I therefore believe it is wrong to give praise on a daily basis, as is proposed by a certain school of thought strongly influenced by the U.S. and as can regularly be found in popular motivation and success literature. Praise is not only the strongest motivator; it is also the one that wears off most rapidly if used in the wrong way.

Not everyone, but most people have a fine sense of whether they are praised rightly or wrongly. They are also aware that they do not deliver a praiseworthy performance every day, just as they know that ordinary performance does not warrant particular praise. A fine sense of these things can be found even in school children.

If a superior gives praise according to what is proposed by so-called modern educational science or in success literature, the people concerned will usually perceive it to be manipulative or even a technique intended to condition them. There is hardly anything more degrading than being subjected to conditioning.

Hence there is only one ground rule that really makes sense: Be sparing with praise! Which also implies: not give praise for simple, ordinary things.

People do not usually expect to be praised for the work they have contractually committed and are paid to do. Of course, we all like the occasional kind word, but no one will have a serious problem if that kind remark is not forthcoming. Praise is appropriate and necessary for truly outstanding performance, for what people do in excess of their contractual duties, and for extraordinary achievements.

Of course there are also people who need praise on a daily basis, who lack the sense of whether they have deserved special recognition or not. These people, however, should not be used as a measure for praise as such; they even constitute a serious problem to any organization. They make it virtually impossible to manage and achieve good performance; they are a strain on the working climate and a problem for everyone else at the workplace, especially when it comes to treating people equally. At bottom, they are a perpetual, personified claim for privileged treatment. It is something that no organization can endure in the long run. This is why people like these should never be a considered benchmark.

Even the most powerful means of motivation will wear off over time, and will essentially lead to an infantilized organization.

Performance Limits

How much can a person accomplish – what are the limits to human performance? We have yet to find an answer to this question and perhaps we will never have one. However, history itself is proof that people can accomplish much more than would have ever been thought possible. The limits are never where people hastily – and often all too willingly – assume them to be.

At the same time, the way in which people are raised, formed, and educated makes it difficult to live by this insight.

Sometimes, artificial limits are set in an attempt to preserve the status quo, hold on to perceived vested rights, and maintain the current balance of power. Some limits result from an ideological aversion to performance, from a tendency to level down differences, and above all, from moral cowardice masked as philanthropy.

The fact that people have exceeded their limits nevertheless, against all obstacles, ought to make us all the more optimistic with regard to their performance potential.

Yet in business, the field that historically has played the pioneer role for performance and performance orientation, we are seeing more limits erected these days than eliminated. It is not done on purpose but because some basic realities are no longer understood. They have been suppressed by a fashionable humanism in education and training which is merely feigned. Artificial and entirely unnecessary limits result, firstly, from motivation theory. Secondly, limits are also set by most efforts in personality development, almost always focusing on the wrong point: on eliminating deficits.

Let me explain this a bit further, using motivation theory as an example – or what has been made of it in management education and training. It has become a piece of conventional wisdom that goes largely unchallenged that people only work and perform when they are motivated. The conclusion many people draw from that is that there is only a need (or justification) to work and perform when the person concerned is motivated. Which, in turn, leads to another logical conclusion: There is a natural claim to being motivated and there will be no performance unless that claim is satisfied: "I don't feel so great today; come on, motivate me!"

Perhaps people have forgotten where and when the general interest in questions of motivation has begun – which was in the U.S., as late as in the 1950s. No one seems to wonder how things used to be before, or in other parts of the world. Before, and outside the wealthy United States, no one could afford the luxury of thinking about motivation. The word itself did not even exist, and neither did the problem. The sources of work and performance were certain value concept, and above all sheer necessity.

People did not work because it felt so good but because they had to and because they considered it their duty. These necessities have not vanished in the developed economies, but they have been diminished and largely replaced by the welfare systems. That in itself may be something to be appreciated. However, one effect of it was that the notions of duty and obligation went astray. Nowadays, anyone appealing to people's sense of duty can be sure to be dismissed as reactionary.

People who get active only when in the mood, and when it suits them well – in other words: when they are motivated – will feel little impulse to exceed or even explore limits once their motivation has ended. Exploring limits is usually hard work; it takes a lot of effort and struggle, sometimes even the kind of extraordinary commitment that may appear superhuman, and which proves and has always proved that man is capable of more things than he himself or those around him would believe.

This becomes particularly obvious in times of crisis, misery, and war – it is unbelievable what people have been able to accomplish and endure in situations like that. And not only there. Anyone interested (and refusing to be put off by all the whining going on in motivation theories) will find outstanding examples in any place and time: in arts and sciences, business and politics, hospitals and families, schools and churches.

People go beyond their perceived limits when they do not stop to wonder whether they are motivated or whether they will be rewarded with an increase in pleasure, but instead feel called upon to perform a task, master a situation, do their duty. In situations like these, nothing could be more ridiculous, meaningless, and cynical than wondering about motivation or pleasure.

This thought may seem old-fashioned today, now that motivation theories have been firmly lodged in so many people's minds. However, it does not take much analysis to find that a society would not be able to function if everyone only did what they felt motivated to do. So, instead of disseminating motivation theories which appear senseless on closer inspection, people had better be encouraged not to pay too much attention to their motivation but to make use of their abilities and strengths as best they can.

Another example of unnecessary limits, and of people being discouraged from exploring them, is what in management we refer to as personality development (in the broadest sense). It is largely based on identifying weaknesses and attempting to eliminate them.

These days we have access to the most sophisticated methods for recognizing people's weaknesses and deficits. Human resources management and professional training are hardly imaginable without them. It is for this very reason that we seem to overlook the fact that people can never become successful by eliminating their weaknesses but only by developing and leveraging their existing strengths.

The misguided philosophy of eliminating weaknesses, which is very popular and appears to be so humane, is not conducive to people's development. In fact, not only does it *not* help people – it even hampers them. It limits their possibilities to even explore their limits, let alone exceed them. Those attempting to eliminate their weaknesses, often in a superhuman effort, rarely achieve more than mediocrity. Usually they end up physically or mentally exhausted, at the very point where others without those weaknesses have effortlessly begun. The effort is enormous – the result is pathetic.

All major accomplishments – in sports, in arts and sciences, in business and in politics – are the result of making rigorous use of one's existing strengths. They have been achieved by people who were encouraged, by others or by themselves, to disregard their weaknesses rather than struggle to eliminate them, and to make the most of the talents which have been given to them.

Burnout and Stress

The media regularly publish lengthy accounts of managers suffering from burnout syndrome and stress. The diagnosis is quickly made and there is no shortage of suggested therapies. Remarkably, despite all the interesting comments made, the most important factor is missing. Could it be that the – usually very young – journalists writing about the subject have very limited first-hand knowledge? Is it possible that they apply the wrong method – asking questions instead of observing what is really happening? And could it be that, above all, they talk to the wrong people – the amateurs among the managers, most of whom fail precisely because they have not achieved an adequate level of professionalism, and who cling to any kind of fad just in order to have an excuse?

So we learn about the agonies suffered by managers, and about the angst that keeps eating away at them… For the umpteenth time we read yet another verbose description of the phenomenon of stress, with all its physical and emotional manifestations; and for the umpteenth time we find that description to be one-sided because it only deals with the negative type of stress – distress – while the positive type, the so-called eustress, is hardly mentioned. Hosts of psychologists, psychoanalysts, and psychotherapists voice their opinions, all certainly very knowledgeable in their fields... and providing yet more evidence of why they had better stick to their trade.

The suggestions put forward are intruiging, sometimes even exciting – all of them regeneration methods of some variety: relaxation, spas, massages, mud baths and herb infusions, exercises in deep-breathing and letting go, personal coaching and empowerment, empathy and learning to listen, networking, recreation, ultimately even emotional intelligence and training in charisma... Fascinating indeed – and usually futile.

Why is it that the simple things are never even mentioned – those that have already proven to be effective? How about the following four suggestions, for a change: Professionalism in fulfilling one's tasks as a result of good management training, a sound personal approach to work, a somewhat stable private life, and regular exercise?

In almost 30 years of working with managers at all levels I have never met anyone who was under stress while these four factors were in place. Many, but not nearly all managers have to work hard, sometimes and in certain phases even too much; occasionally they are in trouble which may sometimes develop into a crisis. They have worries, they do not always feel confident about the decisions they make; they are not always "on the ball", and in the evenings they are sometimes tired.... Well, what else is new? Are other people better off? Are single mothers, surgeons, mountain farmers, students approaching their finals, waiters, sales assistants, detectives or truckers better off?

Good managers do not like talking about themselves. They refuse to complain and they do not publicize what they feel. They concentrate on their duties. They work tirelessly on perfecting their personal approach to work. They have learned from experience that they can keep getting better, and that continuous improvement is enjoyable. They know there are no limits to effectiveness and efficiency, except for those in one's own mind. Instead of being overly sensitive to emotions, they are sensitive to their time and how they use it. They look at the substance rather than the packaging, at facts rather than appearances. They do not waste time on showmanship but work on their craftsmanship instead. They are not interested in rituals but in results, not in input but in output. Most importantly, however, they keep control of their business, they set priorities, and they finish what they have started.

They may be tired in the evening but they do not suffer from burnout. Working effectively, economizing their time, and finishing their tasks: these are their recipes. They enable them to make time for themselves, their families and friends, and the good things in life – maybe not every weekend, but on quite a few weekends. They refuse to give interviews on the subject of stress for two reasons: because they do not suffer from stress and because they do not want to waste their time...

Identification

In many companies, employees are told that they should identify: with the company and its products, with their work, with
the company vision. It sounds plausible enough and many consider it a sign of a particularly modern corporate culture.

I beg to differ. In my view, identification – no matter with
what or whom – is neither necessary nor desirable. This view
runs contrary to mainstream opinion and provokes much opposition. Still, I believe I have good reasons for thinking this way.

Specialist Term or Sloppy Language?

If the subject is discussed with sufficient thoroughness it often
turns out that, fortunately, what is meant is not identification in
the psychological sense. Rather, the expression means that employees should approve of their company, its activities and products, and that they should show commitment.

I certainly agree with that. These are things that management
should be able to expect of people and, logically, a lot has to be
done to enable people to do them.

So is this simply sloppy or ill-considered use of language
rather than a real problem? Well, as long as it does not do any

harm it may be tolerable. However, if anyone really uses the word "identification" in a similar sense as what the psychological term conveys, then that person is treading a dangerous path.

In the psychological sense, identification means: "emotionally equating oneself with another person or group and transferring their or its motives and ideals to one's own self".[8] Do we really want that? May or should we want it?

Against this background, what does it mean when, for example, people are asked to identify with the a company's products? Ninety percent of our domestic product consists of quite ordinary things: foodstuffs, drinks, clothing, consumer electronics, gas pedals, hose clamps. How sick does a person have to be to identify, in the strict sense used in psychology, with mineral water, cheese spread, sausage, credit cards, or MP3 players?

Is it not enough for a person, as an employee, to approve of these things and to be committed to their development, marketing, or sale? Admittedly, employees need to believe in the virtues of a product in order to be able to sell it with conviction. However, being convinced of an item is something entirely different from identifying with it.

Symptoms of Puberty

When do human beings identify with something or someone? I do not know what the reader's experience has been, but I was between 12 and 16 when I identified with the idols und heroes of my time: with the pioneers of rock music, with James Dean,

John F. Kennedy, the German soccer legend Fritz Walter and, being a passionate skier, with the ski racers of my time. I had their photos on my walls and would have gone to the ends of the earth to get an autograph.

The youth of today identify with the idols of their time. At 16, that is a normal and healthy thing to do. However, if a 36-year-old still identifies with idols and heroes, sticking up life-size posters and collecting autographs, then that is questionable and possibly pathological. What in puberty is a symptom of normal development turns into the opposite ten or twenty years later.

No Connection With Performance

Why should people identify with something in the company or with the company itself? There are no convincing indications in relevant literature that identification has anything to do with better performance, or with anything else that could be important to the company.[9]

Managers should enable people to perform in a way that is important to the company, and then allow them to deliver that performance with as little interference as possible. Nothing else is necessary. We pay for the performance, not the reason or motive for it, or for the feelings or emotions connected with it. And even if we wanted to, it is impossible because we have no knowledge of them.

I do not deny that there are reasons and motives which have a positive effect on performance and its quality. Identification is not one of them. Far more important – and also with a longer-lasting effect – are other concepts: a sense of duty, responsibility, commitment, conscientiousness, carefulness.

The most important thing of all is to give people an opportunity to see some meaning or purpose in what they do. As Viktor Frankl, who unfortunately is by far less well-known in management circles than the apostles of identification, repeatedly said in the words of Nietzsche, "He who has a Why to live for can bear with almost any How ..." And he convincingly explains that, when people can no longer see a Why, a meaning, they are indifferent to the How, no matter how wonderful it may be.

Good, effective managers direct their efforts at giving people a task the sense of which they can clearly and distinctly recognize – a task that has some meaning to them. Meaning (in the sense in which Victor Frankl interprets the term) is the key motivator, and the most enduring and effective one at that – and measured by that standard, everything else is far less important.[10]

Loss of Objectivity

One final argument, and the most important one in the management context, is this: identification in the psychological sense is generally connected with a loss of the ability to think critically and to judge with due consideration. Anyone identifying with somebody or something loses any detachment from that object of identification. In this way, he loses the most important prerequisite for any sort of objective power of judgment.

That, however, is the very thing that we ought to expect of managers: enough detachment to be able to think clearly and judge with due consideration. There is no such thing as ultimate and absolute objectivity; but we can create the conditions that make a greater or lesser degree of objectivity possible.

As a chief executive, I want to be surrounded by colleagues and employees who are capable of saying: "Something has been going wrong here lately; we need to change a few things …"

Anyone identifying with someone else or something is unable to do that. He or she becomes a yes person – an employee that is easy to manage but not much help. He agrees with everything, and may even be enthusiastic about it, but he is not a manager. In fact, that person is dangerous.

Risk Appetite

Before a decision is taken, one should always know the risks involved and correctly estimate their impact according to their specific nature.

Rarely before has there been as insistent a call for entrepreneurs and managers with a penchant for risk. It seems that many people consider the enterprising, creative, visionary, risk-taking, dynamic pioneer personality to be the driving force on the way to a new economy. It is currently considered the formula of choice for enabling a Europe which is supposedly falling behind to keep up with the United States and the reviving countries of Asia. In the big corporations, the call may be for the intrapreneur instead of the entrapreneur. Above all, however, it has been going out to founders of start-ups and managers of up-and-coming firms.

But what is it that is demanded of them? Are entrepreneurs and managers really happy to take on risks? And if so, what sort of entrepreneurs and managers – the good ones or the bad? The ones who have already shown they can successfully survive two or three crises, or the ones who go bankrupt or turn into takeover candidates the moment unforeseen difficulties crop up? The New Economy nonsense has shown how little the phenomenon of risk is actually understood. Few things have caused more harm than the lack of understanding of risk and the call for risk appetite.

Good entrepreneurs have a decidedly ambivalent attitude towards risk. They know that there cannot be such a thing as entrepreneurial success without risks; they also know, however, that it is always the risks that drive a company into decline. Hence they have learnt to clearly distinguish between different types of risk.[12] There are four of them, and we need to be careful to keep them separate from one another.

First, there is the risk that all business activity inevitably and always involves. Life itself is perilous, as we all know, and business certainly has no shortage of risks. They are far greater than most people can fathom, because in today's (welfare) society it is virtually impossible to have experiences of that kind. In business, nothing is certain. At the end of every financial year, no matter how good the annual accounts have been, all registers are set back to zero and the struggle and strife start all over.

People who have to draw up balance sheets – in particular those who have to do it with their own money – know that. No one needs to tell them, and that is why they are skeptical about the call for greater risks. That has nothing to do with a lack of entrepreneurial courage, contrary to what so many "economic observers" think. Even the ordinary risk of doing business is high enough: it involves the perpetual risk of going bankrupt.

The *second* type of risk is the additional risk, which, although it exceeds the first, can still be afforded. The reason is that if the blow falls it will not be fatal. This is the sort of risk that people usually take on – and the majority of entrepreneurs will not need a special invitation. If someone makes a hundred thousand per year and takes a thousand to the gambling table, he will probably lose the money but will not be ruined by that loss. What that person actually risks, of course, is not a thousand but two thousand because he has to pay taxes, too. But with that sort of income, even that is something one can get over.

The *third* kind of risk is the kind that once again exceeds the first but definitely cannot be afforded – because it will be a fatal blow if the risk event comes true, because it will drive the company into bankruptcy. This is a risk one should never take, under any circumstances, no matter how great the rewards and regardless of what others may say.

Even the most elaborate theories and calculations, some of them allegedly scientific are of no help here – least of all the determination of probabilities. The question that must be asked is not: How probable is it that the risk event will occur? Rather, it ought to be: What situation will I find myself in if the risk event will occur – no matter how low the probability?

That is not to say that business of this kind should never ever be taken into consideration. However, rather than racking one's brains about probabilities, one should think about how the risk of the third kind can be turned into one of the second kind: by drafting the contract accordingly, by working with partners, or by finding some fool who will shoulder the risk – as many bankers have done in the real-estate field, in hedge fund financing, or in the venture capital sector.

Finally, there is a *fourth* type of risk: the risk that a person cannot afford *not* to take, the risk that *has* to be taken because there is no other choice. This risk, however, cannot be called an entrepreneurial or calculated risk. It is called fate, hopelessness, or tragedy. The Greek tragedies and many of Shakespeare's dramas are built around this form of risk. It makes them thrilling, fascinating and – well, tragic. It is something we like to watch – in theater shows, not in our own companies. This last type of risk is usually the result of earlier mistakes and a failure to heed the unbending principles of management and of doing business. After having thoughtlessly said A, B, and C years ago, one is now forced to accept X, Y, and Z.

At least these four kinds of risks should be distinguished – in particular by those who so loudly call for the risk-loving entre-preneur, often from an entirely risk-free position. No one bene-fits from a corporate insolvency, except for the lawyers handling it; it always implies the destruction of productive power and wealth. Above all, commitment and entrepreneurial motivation are destroyed when young people are inveigled by seductive slo-gans to take risks of the wrong kind, allured by seductive slo-gans.

Fun

Should work be fun? Does it have to be fun? Today, the answer to these questions is mostly yes. And what else should it be? Yet however plausible this may seem, it is actually problematic because it is generally understood to be a demand or claim, rather than a wish.

This claim has become a dominant idea in management and management training – with disastrous repercussions. It has given rise to expectations that no company can fulfill in the long run.

Unrealistic Expectations

The demand for fun is one of the false doctrines that make it impossible to motivate staff sensibly. It sets off a vicious circle: the expectations built up by managers and trainers are not met, which is bound to frustrate employees; management responds by initiating motivational programs and "motivating" behaviors; under the given circumstances, however, employees cannot help but perceive these efforts as attempted manipulation or even a particularly refined form of cynicism, because usually the nature of the work does not change and all the demands for pleasure and fun remain unsatisfied.

This is bound to further increase the general frustration, as people now feel they have been "taken for a ride". Getting out of this vicious circle is only possible if one finds the courage to adopt a new attitude of realism and begins to describe things as they are.

More Differentiation

First off, remember that this is the first time in history that the demand for fun at work has been raised. That will not eliminate the demand as such, but it may be a suitable way to put it into perspective. Second, it is useful to distinguish between fun and pleasure. They are not the same, which is why language has two separate terms for them.

It goes without saying that every effort should be made to eliminate any suffering associated with work, wherever possible; the developed economies have seen considerable progress in this respect over the past 100-odd years. This is one of those revolutions whose history has yet to be written. It also goes without saying that it is great progress if, at least from time to time, more and more forms of work can also provide pleasure or fun.

At the same time, it must be made unequivocally clear that no job can be pleasurable all the time and that practically any kind of work has aspects which can never bring pleasure to anybody. It would be naïve to claim otherwise.

Even professions that are generally believed to be ideal, exciting and fascinating, like perhaps that of a pilot or orchestral conductor, have their tedious sides. Even they involve a growing amount of routine and drudgery over time.

It must also be said very clearly that there are jobs which need to be done and which, apart from including cumbersome elements, will usually not bring pleasure or fun to anybody. There will still be toilets to be cleaned in the future, we will still need garbage collectors, and there will still be plenty of unskilled jobs. What are these people supposed to gain from the motto that work should be fun?

The idea of fun must be equally questionable to those whose job brings them face to face with the suffering of the world every day: refugee aid workers who cannot provide any real help; social workers unable to eliminate drug addiction, prostitution or homelessness; teachers and priests in the slums of major cities; doctors and nurses whose work in intensive care is hopeless too often. They do their work not because of the pleasure but because it has to be done – even if that may sound old-fashioned to some people.

Work or Results?

The claim that work should be pleasure and fun leads not only to intractable problems of motivation. It has another negative consequence: it distracts attention from the most important thing that must be associated with work – the results. It draws people's attention to the work itself instead of directing it onto the results of their work. It is not the work itself that matters, it is the achievement – not the input but the output. It is therefore important to talk not just about unemployment but also about underachievement.

The claim, if one really wants to raise it, would better be expressed as follows: it is not the task that should bring pleasure but its results. Although that does not always work, it is sometimes possible even if the work itself is absolutely no fun. In those cases, the results achieved can still bring pleasure or at least provide a hint of satisfaction. Work results can be associated with justifiable pride, which provides even those people who have to perform the simplest unskilled jobs with the minimum of self-respect that every human being needs.

If people have jobs that give them fun or pleasure they can consider themselves lucky. It is a privilege in every respect and a rarity. If all jobs were stopped except those that are fun, society would be at a standstill within twelve hours. As long as this largely holds true, expressions like duty and conscientiousness should not be removed from our vocabulary, even if they are not in line with the zeitgeist.

Management Errors

Management Style

There is hardly a workshop or training where no one asks questions about management style. It has been one of the most-discussed issues of the past decades. In hardly another field has there been so much empirical research, and there is hardly a manager who has not dealt with the subject. It is a central topic in every management training because everyone involved believes it to be so important.

I take a contrary position. I consider the subject to be largely insignificant, or at least much less significant than it is generally believed to be. My view contradicts conventional wisdom, and I have two reasons for it.

No Correlation

Firstly, there is no correlation between management style and results. It is possible to create such correlations in a laboratory or training environment – every trainer knows exercises to achieve this; they are standard in the business training scene and useful to facilitate insights and learning effects. They are, however, not applicable to everyday business reality.

Everyone knows managers who practice a cooperative management style, and who also achieve outstanding results. It goes without saying and does not need to be commented that this is an ideal situation. On the other hand, there are managers practicing authoritarian leadership and producing poor results. In that case, it is equally clear that the situation is unacceptable and their organization will have to let them go. Both of these variants do not warrant any further discussion.

But how about the less obvious cases? I know several managers who practice a truly cooperative management style, who strike others as pleasant and well-mannered, but who unfortunately fail to produce satisfactory results. And I know managers whose controlling and rigid style has earned them a reputation for being rather authoritarian – but who present good results on a regular basis. If I was to choose between the two, I would prefer the latter.

It is the results that count, not the style. Management is the profession of effectiveness, or, in other words, of producing results. If it can be done in a cooperative manner, all the better. If not, results must be given priority over style.

People lacking management practice often find that hard to accept. Those looking back at a few years of practical experience will usually agree. But even they will often find it difficult to put that knowledge to practice. What they lack is not insight, but the courage to challenge a dogma of management theory, and perhaps even throw it overboard.

What Matters Is Manners

My second point is: What matters is not style but something else – something hardly ever mentioned in management training: it is manners, or what you might call a sense of decency or propriety. Whenever I express this opinion, opportunistic trainers will tell me that that is exactly what they mean when they talk about style. Style and manners are two entirely different things, though.

When I say "manners" I am not referring to fancy, artfully cultivated rituals of politeness. I am talking about a person's bearing, about such simple things as saying "please" and "thank you" to one's assistants, even those at the lowest ranks; about hearing people out and really listening to them – perhaps not for hours but certainly attentively; about not interrupting them and not yelling at them; about not showing one's moods, no matter how bad one may feel; about not taking out one's negative feelings on others.

These are things we are taught from childhood on. If as a manager you encounter people who obviously have not learnt them, you will have no choice but demand that they adopt them for the workplace. Compromises are not permissible. Rude behavior must not be tolerated.

All of the aforesaid has nothing to do with style. It is about correct behavior. As a manager it is your duty to behave correctly toward your staff at all times. The same is true for colleagues – something which, lamentably, seems not to be self-evident – and it is also true for your behavior toward your superiors, which usually goes without saying. A lack of manners cannot be compensated with style. Anyone lacking in manners but trying to deal with his staff in a "cooperative way" will risk being perceived as a "suck-up" and an opportunist.

No Career for Boors

Under Alfred P. Sloan – who headed General Motors from 1920 to 1956, making it the world's largest company for quite a while and the most profitable of its time – no one would get ahead if he lacked basic manners. Sloan himself was extremely correct in these matters. At the same time, he did show rigor whenever necessary – and he needed to: initially because he was faced with the competitive superiority of Ford, and later to get the company through hard times.

Sloan was highly esteemed and respected, not only because of his entrepreneurial achievements but because he never failed to adhere to the basic principles of human decency. This has nothing to do with what is nowadays referred to as "corporate culture"; however, a corporate culture only deserves the name if it is rooted in those very principles of decency.

According to a law of physics, there is friction when solid bodies make contact. Organizations are places where "solid bodies" (people) make contact – so there is "friction" (conflict). And while good manners cannot be the fuel, the energy to drive an organization forward, they are the "lubricant" – the substance that makes friction bearable. People have rough edges; there is no way to set up an organization in such a way that it will be 100 percent conflict-free, just as there is no way to design an engine to be 100 percent friction-free.

In the absence of conflict there is no reason to train managers in conflict management. In fact, it should never be one of the first subjects taught in management trainings. The purpose of such trainings should be to create an understanding of management that will not give rise to conflict. In other words, the managers' task is not so much to resolve conflict but to treat their people in such a way that conflict can be avoided. And one of the chief prerequisites for that is manners.

Note that I have not used the words "protocol" and "etiquette" here. Whether a manager is capable of determining a seating order in accordance with the rules of higher diplomacy, or whether he knows how to eat lobster properly, are questions of secondary interest. Protocol and etiquette do have their significance, and the higher your position the less you can ignore them. But only in the rarest of cases do they play a key role in practical everyday management. Manners and decency do. They are indispensable conditions without which there cannot be reasonable management, particularly in areas where demanding brainwork is required. They are much cheaper than any training in leadership style and conflict management, let alone a restructuring effort. They are also much more effective. And they can be established much more easily than anything else.

Leadership

One of the risky words that have been spreading in recent years is "leadership", and the most dangerous of all is "leader". These words are dangerous because they relate to both the best and the worst deeds in history. They can be misused too easily.

My meaning would immediately become clear if the equivalent German terms were used: they are the words that made the 20th century the bloodiest in the history of mankind. The 21st century has not begun with exemplary leadership either, rather with its opposite. Even fifty years' distance from the worst misuse of the terms "Führer" and "Führerschaft" are not enough – using them in discussion will still provoke protest.

In certain combinations the word "leadership" is harmless and can hardly be misunderstood: for instance, there are no problems with market leadership or cost leadership in either English or German. Where the word is objectionable is in connection with wrong translations – this time from German to English, which has become the corporate language in many German companies.

The German word "Führung" would hardly be translated as "leadership" when referring to a company or business: the correct translation in almost all instances is "management". The word "Führungskraft" (the person performing that task) would be translated as "manager", lately also quite often as "executive", particularly when referring to higher-ranking people. In certain contexts another possibility would be "head of ..." – but never "leader".

The dangerousness of the word "leadership" is apparent in two cases which have lately become more and more frequent: when it is used in a certain comparative sense, contrasting it with "management", and when it is linked with the demand for a certain type of personality.

In current literature, most authors writing about leadership show a marked tendency to sharply distinguish between management and leadership. In order to enhance the importance of leadership, they play down the significance of management.

According to them, managers are mere administrators, operatives, and executants, clinging to the given state of things, focused on the present, working with rules and controls – in other words, bureaucrats to the core – whereas leaders are innovators, exciting visionaries and pioneers.

The head of training at one of the largest banks of Switzerland's put it this way: "Leadership creates real change, whereas management only initiates small changes."

Someone else distinguished between the "transforming leader" and the manager by ascribing to them qualities like the following:

Leader	Manager
Wide	Narrow
Deep	Superficial
Experimental	Mechanical

Active	Reactive
Long-term	Short-term
Flexible	Rigid
Open	Closed

Of course, everyone is free to describe things as they please. The only question is what they gain by doing that. The mere fact that there are people in management positions to whom the terms on the right-hand side apply says absolutely nothing about management. It merely proves that there are positions which are filled with the wrong people.

I would like to propose something entirely different: If we want to try to recognize, analyze, and perhaps even teach and learn – if at all possible – what the real essence of leadership is, we will need to start with a positive understanding of management and from there go on to ask what leadership comprises above and beyond that. Otherwise we will simply refer to everything bad as management and to everything good as leadership. In other words, we will have exchanged some terms for others and shuffled some words around, but we will not have learnt anything about leadership.

There are countless future-looking, visionary and innovative managers who meet all the criteria defining leaders but are far too modest to call themselves leaders or allow others to call them that. They would fit it presumptuous. To them, it is enough to be considered good managers.

The use of the word "leadership" becomes particularly dangerous when, as regularly happens, it is coupled with a call for a particular type of personality: the outstanding, extraordinary, charismatic, missionary elite individual, destined by fate to be a leader. That is a simplistic and historically short-sighted way of thinking, and it fails to accomplish the most fundamental purpose that any reasonable leadership theory should accomplish: distinguishing leaders from misleaders, and genuine leaders from egomaniacs, bluffers, and autocrats.

Images of Man

Almost every important aspect of management – such as motivation, performance, satisfaction, values, corporate culture – seems to depend on an underlying concept of man and on the correct use of the respective term. This is dangerous because it gives rise to rigid ideas about people, precisely where we would need flexibility.

The discussion keeps returning to the same two typifications which the American psychologist Douglas McGregor referred to as "Theory X" and Theory Y" in his book "The Human Side of Enterprise", first published in 1960. Even back then these two concepts of man were as old as the hills; variations of them can be found throughout the history of thought. For management they are largely useless since they cause more damage than they add value.

One concept – Theory X – depicts man as a weak creature in need of help, dependent on the solidarity of his community, incapable of shaping his life and of taking responsibility for it; a creature that perceives work to be painful and troublesome, which is why he tends to avoid it and has to be motivated by others, and who is in need of "salvation", as it were. The other concept – Theory Y – portrays man as a strong and capable being that motivates himself, likes to work and perform and does so voluntarily, a being that makes his own decisions and controls his life, and who finds purpose and self-fulfillment in doing exactly that.

Refuse to Typecast People

Whichever of these two images of man one may lean towards, my suggestion is to absolutely and totally dispense with any image of man for the purposes of management. Of course, none of us is totally free of assumptions and opinions; however, I recommend actively refusing to have any image of man, as it can lead into the trap of cliché and prejudice. Admittedly, this is not always easy – but we are dealing with management and managers here, and they can certainly be expected to make something of an effort.

It is best to begin by accepting that we do not know what human beings in general are like. Of the six billion or so human beings that currently populate the world, no two are the same. We are all unique individuals.

But do we have to know what human beings are like? Fortunately, in management no one is faced with the problem of having to manage all human beings at once – only the eight, ten or twelve people that fate, chance or one's own choice has brought together as one's direct reports. Hence one only needs to know what these few people are like. And that is something that can be found out, even if science will never discover anything that is universally true about the motivation of human beings.

Find Out What the Individual Is Like

I do not mean to preach the virtues of being free of prejudice, as desirable as this may be. Rather, I am pursuing a very practical purpose. If we refuse to accept a general image of man and if we accept that we do not know what human beings in general are like, the logical consequence is that we need to find out what the individual we have to work with is like. Anyone doing that will probably find that no one conforms to a general image of man.

Imagine an employee who seems to be a "Theory X type" at work, apparently thinking of nothing else but the end of the working day. Yet in his leisure time he devotes himself with much commitment and motivation to a responsible function at a club or society, a charitable organization or a political party, or he is passionate in his pursuit of a hobby or sport. In the company he only does what he absolutely has to, but whenever there is a community run he is sure to be there. So what kind of person is he? Or take someone who does a splendid job at work and is clearly a "Theory Y type", but who is never up to much in his leisure time and spends his evenings watching TV. How should he be categorized? X types do not always show X behavior and Y types do not always deliver Y performance.

There are people who have periods of strong performance but then "sag" for days or weeks, just hanging around and keeping in an almost depressive state. Many people "don't feel up to much" on Mondays; on Tuesdays they begin shaping up; on Wednesdays they accomplish something special which sends their motivation soaring; on Thursdays something goes wrong; and on Fridays most people – among them quite a few top managers – already start thinking about the weekend. What concept of man do these people fit into? Some are simple-minded when young and grow cleverer as they get older; for others the opposite is true. The most impressive examples, which are not even that rare, are those of people who surpass themselves when faced with a special task, after everyone else had doubted they would ever be capable of achieving much.

Every sports coach has learnt not to pay attention to types but to look at the individual performance profile of each athlete. Anyone fixated on concepts of man runs the risk of doing people injustice and, what is more, he neglects what is most important in management: finding out what each individual person is capable of, what strengths and potential he has, and putting him where he can make a real difference.

Staffing Decisions

Successful corporate management is based on two foundations: role models at the top and good staffing decisions. Both are indispensable; both bear no compromise. Staffing decisions are the ultimate means of managing an organization. There is no need for sophisticated methods, although they are precisely what fascinates many people. (This is how you can tell dilettantes from capable managers.) In fact, what is required is diligence and strict adherence to some basic principles. More than ever before, the risk of wrong staffing decisions became apparent from the mistakes made in the 1990s and more recently.

The first principle is: No one is an expert in human nature. Even if some find this hard to believe: Truly experienced people do not rely on their judgment of character, even if they consider it to be one of their strengths. Intuition and first impressions are bad advisors. The risk involved in staffing decisions is too big to base them on subjective certainty.

The second principle is: Anyone hiring the wrong people has to bear the responsibility. The second principle refers to correcting wrong staffing decisions. For each lame duck in a given position there is someone who put him there. That is who has to take the responsibility and to correct his earlier decision – not the person that failed. The famous "Peter principle", according to which everyone is promoted until he reaches his personal level of incompetence, is nothing but a handy excuse for a lack of diligence.

The third principle is: A quick staffing decision is usually a wrong decision. Due to their significance, their longevity, their precedent and signal effect, staffing decisions – in particular for senior positions – must be taken with all the care, diligence, and thoroughness imaginable and humanly possible. It takes time, and decision-makers need to take that time.

The fourth principle is: Never entrust a rookie with a task that is new and critical for the organization. New and critical tasks must only be given to people you know and whom you can judge. People you do not really know yet must be given other assignments. If you break this rule you will face an equation with two unknowns, thus taking on incalculable risks. In most cases it is possible to abide by this rule, but it hits a brick wall when top positions must be filled with candidates from outside the company. This is usually one of the riskiest situations imaginable and it should be avoided as far as possible.

The fifth principle is: There are no universal geniuses. In particular when it comes to filling elevated positions, people easily fall into a very specific trap: that of the universal genius. They go looking for a "multi-talent", an "all-rounder". The universal genius, however, is a fiction, a legend, the protagonist on the stage of bad management theories. He can be characterized but never found. Having accepted that fact, some fall into the opposite trap: They select the candidates with the fewest deficits – the "well-rounded personality". The former mistake results in a quest for the impossible, the latter leads straight into mediocrity.

The secret of every organization lies neither in "universal geniuses" nor in "well-rounded personalities". It lies in people with exactly the strengths that the organization, in its specific situation, needs to be successful. If a company faces a period of innovation it will need people with strengths in that field; in a turnaround situation it will need different skills and capabilities.

It is a rule of nature that strengths always occur in conjunction with weaknesses. Experienced and successful managers are aware of that. They will focus on the strengths and accept the weaknesses that come with them – often, many and major ones. And while they cannot eliminate these weakness, in the end they become meaningless in view of the results achieved with the strengths.

Teamwork

Two of the most notorious buzzwords today are "team" and "teamwork". Those particularly keen on conforming to the zeitgeist portray them as the polar opposite of individual achievement, which embodies everything that is bad and "out", whereas teamwork is good and "in". Teamwork has been one of the most frequently used terms in management for some time. Almost without exception, the word is meant positively; teams and teamwork are regarded not merely as one of several forms of work but as the only desirable one. In principle and in general, teams are considered to be superior to the individual. They are viewed as being good, efficient, creative and successful per se. All of this sounds very nice. Unfortunately, though, there is not a shred of evidence that this assumption is correct.

I am not saying there is no need for teamwork, but this has always been the case. What is so new about it that it requires special emphasis; and what makes it so difficult that it must be learnt and practised separately? How can anyone justify the dogmatism associated with it, which chooses to see it as the only form of useful work?

What Is So Difficult About Teamwork?

Ever since humans have existed, cooperation has been a matter of course in daily life. What is called a team today is the basic form of any social structure whatsoever. It is virtually the constitutive element of society: the cooperation of people in various different ways in order to cope with life, be it the diverse forms of family, the prehistoric pack of hunters, the tribal community, the rural farming community, the handicraft business, the village community and so forth. Nobody could have survived without cooperation; Robinson Crusoe is just a fiction.

For this reason, it was never a problem for anybody to work in and as a team with others. Nobody needed to be taught; nobody needed to learn it. Life as such happened in teams; life was teamwork. Hence teamwork, and what has lately been referred to as social skills, has scarcely received a mention from historians. Never have I come across passages such as "… and then the Assyrians invented the team …"

What, then, are the changes that seem to require one of the most mundane facts of life of the past millenia to be considered so important? And above all, what has made it so difficult that it has to be studied and that it is now a criterion for making a career, even for being of any use professionally? Have people suddenly become social illiterates and cretins at communication? Are so many of us autistic?

I hardly think so. Perhaps, as a result of certain ideologically motivated school projects, we now have some more people in our organizations who have never learnt how to finish things alone because they were hiding in study or experience groups too often. Perhaps we also have more of those who never experienced first-hand the difference between success and failure at school, because they were never really assessed and they therefore considered it an achievement to even finish school. Certain questionable trends in education have left their marks, and people affected by them now have to struggle to fill certain gaps. They are a minority, though.

Yet what we are increasingly confronted with today are senseless forms of organization and impracticable types of labor division, which prevent almost any productive work or make it inhumanly difficult at any rate. For example, anybody who has to work in a matrix organisation – most of which have been introduced too quickly, indiscriminately and without proper consideration – must have an extraordinary level of teamwork skill, to an extent that is rarely found and can usually not be created by any amount of training. It is therefore much better, more effective and more economical to modify the organization.

The purpose of organization is not to make work difficult for people. On the contrary, it is supposed to make it easy. If we stop imposing performance-hindering organizations on people we will quickly find that most of them can work together quite well and without major problems – precisely because that is one of the perfectly normal abilities of ordinary people, and there is no particular need to train people for teamwork.

It would hardly occur to anyone to make a nonsensical demand for teamwork when people drive a car, play a musical instrument, or compete at chess. We all know that these tasks, if they are to stand the slightest chance of success and efficiency or even brilliance, can be performed by individuals only and that no amount of team training would lead to even so much as mediocre achievements. Of course the performance of a symphony requires teamwork; no musician needs to be told. But this does not mean that the trumpet is blown by a team. And it is for a reason that even the most difficult and demanding of instruments, the organ, is constructed in such a way that it can only be played by one organist alone.

If one were to configure the positions and tasks in management with the same care exercised by the great composers in writing the different voices of a symphony, teamwork would not be an issue – or to be more precise: it could be relied upon that ordinary people quite naturally bring with them everything they need to work together. Teamwork would be no problem.

Yet no amount of training will achieve the opposite: to compensate for mistakes in job designs and organization structures through team training.

So What About Truly Great Accomplishments?

The things that people need to be able to do in order to work together can thus be assumed as given under sensible conditions. But what about truly outstanding accomplishments? Might real excellence, the great creative breakthrough, perhaps be a matter for the team? Would the ordinary teamwork skill of ordinary people still be sufficient for that task? Or is this the point where special training is required?

The thought is fascinating enough to check whether it holds water. Whether or not we will find the result surprising depends on our familiarity with the activities and achievements of those we refer to as "great" characters.

Virtually all major achievements, especially those commonly

referred to as breakthroughs, were accomplished by individual people, sometimes by individuals with assistants, but almost never by teams. This is true of all the different forms of art: neither are there musical compositions nor any works of literature that were produced by teams; neither do we know of teams of painters nor did any of the great sculptors really work in a team.[13]

Contrary to widespread opinion this is equally true for science, so it should be taken seriously. The great works of philosophy, mathematics, the sciences and the humanities were, with few exceptions, created by individuals. This is occasionally concealed by certain ways of quoting and by conventions in the context of the Nobel Prize award, but it can be proved for a sufficient number of cases.

Teamwork is a method, as is individual performance. Neither of the two should be dismissed entirely, neither should be put on a pedestal. Exactly how something should be done and which form of work is the best is something to be determined by the particular task and not by dogmas.

In the world of organizations, tasks must be designed in such a way that they can be performed by ordinary people (because there is no other kind) who have ordinary abilities (because others are not learnable).

Companies that want to achieve results have to master both: teamwork and the individual achievement, each where it fits best. Anyone out to make a career for himself – or rather, anyone wishing to perform well and consistently – who, as a manager, has to rely on the trust and respect of other people, ought to refuse to work with catchphrases and to be taken in by fads and fashions.

Vision

One of the most fashionable words of the past two decades, and at the same time one of the most dangerous ones, is "vision". Its emergence is largely owed to poor translations from English to other languages. I suggest not using the word "vision" at all in a company. It does much more damage than it serves a useful purpose.

The vast majority of recent corporate collapses in the banking and insurance sector, in telecommunications and in the media industry are almost entirely attributable to the fact that the term "vision" was allowed to proliferate unchecked. This includes virtually all of the start-ups of the stock exchange boom years, which had nothing to offer apart from visions. But visions impress people.

What is good about the word and what is dangerous? I do not deny that managers have to be capable of formulating some idea of future developments, that they have to look beyond the narrow confines of the business as it currently is, that they need to show foresight and imagination. That has always been the case, in particular for the people we like to refer to as "leaders".

They, however, managed to do without the word "vision". We do not find it in Churchill or Napoleon, in Mahatma Gandhi or Frederick the Great. We also look for it in vain among the great founders of companies and tycoons like Alfred Krupp, August Thyssen, J.P. Morgan, Henry Ford, and Werner von Siemens. They may have used the term in passing but it certainly did not form a crucial part of their thinking about their future plans.

Up until the early 1990s, the standard *Duden* dictionary of the German language, for example, defined vision simply as *"visual or sensory illusion"*, *"optical hallucination"*, and *"supernatural apparition constituting a religious experience"*. And for hundreds of years, those were exactly the meanings that the word had. It was only later that the following was added: *"picture formed in a person's mind, in particular with regard to the future"*.

In other words, the linguistic meaning used in management is a rather new one. It has done nothing for the professionalism of management. Hardly anyone will wish to claim that the past ten years' achievements in management have exceeded those of the founding pioneers. The opposite is true: they have not even come anywhere close.

Under the bombastic term "vision", what has been constructed is nothing but castles in the air and houses of cards which collapsed at the slightest puff of economic "wind". Looking at it that way, one could even say that the term was well chosen. Of course, that was not what the people who created and used it had in mind.

It is not simply a question of semantics and certainly not one of hair-splitting. The problem is much more serious. Vision, as a fashion, accorded attention and recognition to certain personality types who, at one time, would have had no chance in a well-managed company: the bluffers and boasters, the dreamers and charlatans. By indicating how important vision was and by pointing to management literature of a certain type, it was possible to give a semblance of legitimacy and importance even to the most arrant nonsense. Even worse, the bluffers could evade all critical discussion by belittling the skeptics and critics and reproaching them for their lack of vision. Empty rhetoric and denunciation were able to take the place of the serious discussion that would have been more helpful.

The crucial failure is the lack of any distinction between *good* and *bad* vision. In all of the counted books on vision, not once is there an indication on how to distinguish one from the other, how to separate a workable vision from nonsense, or what the difference might be between mere fantasies and usable ideas.

Not only are there no criteria to be found – the problem is not even discussed. When I once asked one of the busiest authors of vision literature how she thought the wheat could be separated from the chaff, she had no answer and became indignant instead. Well, indignation in place of expert knowledge may be something one must occasionally take in one's stride and in polite silence – but it will not solve any problems. Another time, when I asked a professor from a reputable university to provide a definition, the answer readily given was: "*A vision is a dream with a deadline*". A remark like that may come handy as a nice and impressive opening to a lecture, but it is completely useless for any sort of serious work. Every dream has a deadline, and fortunately so does every nightmare...

For all these reasons, I personally prefer terms which have more substance and are more down-to-earth, such as, for instance, business mission, corporate policy objective, or strategic concept. I know they all have their disadvantages and vague elements, but anyone with a sound training in management and who is familiar with the right literature in this field will know exactly what the terms mean. He will go by the content and substance, not by the semantic packaging, and bluffs and charlatans will soon be exposed.

Imagination and bold ideas are certainly one aspect of good management. However, there has to be a clear distinction between good and bad ideas, between those that are useful and those of no use. The excesses of the past years should be example enough to prove my point.

Emotion

These days, anyone demanding "gut instinct" and condemning "braininess" can be sure to be rewarded with general approval, in certain circles even veneration. Different variants of pleas for more "emotionality"[3] in management are always certain to sell well. Even top managers and entrepreneurs are regularly heard calling for more intuition.

Conversely, you are bound to meet with fierce opposition if you do the opposite – if you dare call for less gut instinct and more intellect in a discussion. Even demands to strike a balance between the two are often received with suspicion. The quality of discussion is worthy of the Middle Ages, and so is the dogmatism.

Remarkably, there has not been a single scientific study to demonstrate the superiority of gut instinct over reason, least of all in those areas of management where it is most insistently contended: in observing, comprehending and evaluating complex facts and basing decisions on them – correct decisions.

In fact, studies have shown the very opposite[4]. It is true that people's emotions are a natural part of complex systems – one of the most important, perhaps even *the* most important of their active components. (Hence, for example, the significance of emotions for marketing, politics, and religion.) That is something we need to know and we can make use of – for which, incidentally, an effort of the intellect is needed. Feelings as such, however, are no help in understanding these complex systems and situations, or in dealing with them correctly. One of the crucial obstacles here is the sense of certainty that feelings generally entail.

Only Positive Emotions?

When emotions and their desirable effects in management are mentioned, this usually relates to positive emotions, such as love, compassion, or sympathy. And who would want to be without them? But are they the only ones that exist? Nothing is ever said or written about negative, destructive, bad emotions. What about envy, malevolence, hatred, jealousy and aggression? Would we also want those in our families and organizations, all under the label of "more feeling"? This goes to show that it is not enough simply to call for more emotion.

The development of a civilization, or indeed a culture, very much depends on the human being having learnt to curb and discipline his emotions, instincts and drives.[5] Many emotions are decidedly anti-social. Disciplining such destructive emotions is the central purpose of ethics, morality, law and good manners. Man is a social being only to the degree that he has learnt to follow rules rather than giving in to his urges. He is human not because he has emotions – animals have them, too – but because he has gotten his emotions under control.

This is why, if organizations are to work, it is highly recommendabled that emotions be replaced by propriety. In my 30 years of practical experience I have not seen a single instance where the cause of and/or reason for escalation of a conflict was anything other than emotions. In the private sphere things may be viewed differently; in an organization, emotions – even positive ones – will cause nothing but trouble.

Can Feelings Be Relied On?

How correct are decisions which are based on gut instinct? Leaving aside the error rate of emotional decisions when selecting a partner (think of the divorce rates) and of the "gut" decisions taken on the stock exchange (look at the bottom lines), a few simple tests suffice to reveal the unreliability of judgments and decisions made on the strength of emotions:

For example, outside air-conditioned rooms only few people are capable of estimating temperatures correctly. What is subjectively considered hot or cold turns out to be very different on the thermometer, with its "brainy" objectiveness. Similarly, hardly anyone is capable of making even a roughly accurate estimate of relative humidity or wind speed. And estimates made by passers-by regarding the speed of cars (for instance in the event of a car accident) are so notoriously incorrect that they are considered worthless testimony in court. Something similar is true of estimates referring to time. What is called a "sense of time" is usually so hopelessly off the mark and so greatly affected by the particular situation as to be useless. Ten minutes at the dentist's seem like an eternity, whereas two gripping hours at the movie theater pass in a flash.

Things become questionable when, for example, people are recommended – often quite authoritatively – to "go by their instinct" when it comes to physical exercise. No one is capable of determining his or her pulse rate correctly without a pulse rate monitor, except after years of exercise involving systematic measurements of pulse rates and exact records. Even then the error rate is still high.

In the field of complex systems, Jay Forrester showed in his ground-breaking studies at MIT that complex systems behave in what he called a counter-intuitive manner; so this would systematically make it difficuelt to comprehend, assess and judge them based on gut instinct.

Deficiencies of Human Reason Cannot Be Compensated by Emotion

There is no denying that human reason sometimes fales. However, just why emotions should not suffer from the same deficiency is a question yet unanswered. Regardless of all arguments and refutations, the mere and unsubstantiated claim that emotions are superior to reason stubbornly persists. And while it cannot be proven to be true, it is repeated all the more frequently – usually with a great deal of emotion.

Emotion is blithely given priority over reason and intellect. Emotion is associated with warmth and humanity, reason with their opposites, with coldness and, though not with inhumanity, yet with icy calculation.

This mutually exclusive division people constantly make is wrong and foolish – for the very reason that the logical opposite of rational is not emotional but irrational, and the counterpart of emotional is unemotional, not non-emotional or devoid of emotion.

I am not denying either the existence of feelings or their importance or effect. It is also true that the application of reason always takes place in a context of emotions and thinking processes are always accompanied by emotions. There is no such thing as pure reason; and the philosophy of pure rationalism that advocates it has done enormous damage.

With all the usual shortcomings of human reason, which may be particularly limiting in the individual case, there is no convincing proof that emotions could replace or even supplement reason when it comes to understanding complex systems, making decisions within these systems, or managing them. In my opinion, whoever believes that is being duped by an illusion or by a lack of knowledge of the current state of research.

The mere fact that emotions are ubiquitous and have enormous impact must not be mistaken as proof that they are a reliable means of orientation and navigation. Emotions are seated in a very ancient region of the brain, the so-called limbic system. They may have been reliable in an environment where this region of the brain first developed. However, why this should still be the case today, in an entirely different environment, is something that the proponents of this "theory" fail to explain. Could it be that emotions are actually grossly unreliable? So unreliable, in fact, that only those organisms which have managed to evolve further and to survive while their environment grew increasingly complex developed the cerebrum with its abilities of comprehension and reasoning?[6]

Unfortunately, even questions of this kind cannot keep people from buying and even applauding books that recommend "limbic thinking" (a contradiction in itself) to managers. The statement we find in many of those books is doubtlessly true – managerial decisions are often made "by gut instinct". What they fail to say, however, is that these decisions are often wrong.

The lamentable fact that even brain researchers[7] judge those books positively simply falls into the embarrassment category. It leads us to remind them of the old saying about the cobbler sticking to his last.

Focus

The principle of focus is important everywhere. It has particular significance in management because no other profession is so greatly and systematically exposed to the dangers of dissipation and fragmentation.

These dangers also exist in other fields, but nowhere else are they so institutionalized, so widely accepted and so grossly misunderstood as a sign of particular dynamics and performance. Conversely, nothing is as typical a sign of effectiveness as the capability or the art, or better even: the discipline of focusing.

The word "focus" alone, however, is not enough; it can still be misunderstood. This is why it appears among the "dangerous words": for anyone interested in having impact and success, the key is to focus on few things, on a limited number of carefully selected focal points. Selecting these priorities requires prudence, diligence, careful consideration of one's situation – and practical experience. Hardly anything else is needed, least of all any of the exceptional qualities and capabilities so grandiosely demanded by the management in-crowd.

An occasional objection is that the principle of focus is not applicable in complex and network situations.

The exact opposite is true: the principle is important for the very reason that things are so complex, networked, and interactive. It was less important in the past, simply because it is not needed in straightforward situations: when there is hardly any distraction, thus the principle of focus is automatically applied. Neither the farmer plowing his field nor the worker at the steel plant nor the stonemason of the gothic age was ever exposed to the temptations of distraction that are typical of management positions today, in particular senior ones.

The fact of the matter is clear: while it is possible to occupy oneself with a number of different things at a time, it is not possible to be successful in all of them at once. Consequently, a distinction must be made between work and performance, occupation and achievement.

Wherever there is impact, achievement, and result, we will – if we exclude coincidence and luck – invariably find that the principle of focusing on a limited number of things has been applied. Almost everyone who has come to prominence or even fame through their own achievements has focused on one thing, one task, one problem. It often grew into on obsession, sometimes even verging on the pathological, which is not what I recommend. In all cases, however, concentration on one thing or few things was the key to achieving results. It is crucial even for achieving ordinary results and, without exception and compromise, more so for outstanding, extraordinary results – for excellence.

The importance of this principle has been attested to by people from very different fields, including Albert Einstein and Martin Luther, Bertolt Brecht and Auguste Renoir, Johann Strauß and Ludwig Wittgenstein, Thomas Mann and Jean-Jacques Rousseau.

Most instructive are the examples of people who were both effective and successful despite having to cope with particularly harsh conditions, such as illness, a handicap, or an excessive workload. What invariably becomes evident is that their success is based on applying a strict focus to their work, which their particular circumstances forced them to do. One of the most remarkable and well-documented cases is that of Harry Hopkins. At the time of World War II he was the closest personal advisor to and delegate of President Franklin D. Roosevelt, the gray eminence in Washington, D.C. Despite the fact that he was seriously ill and ultimately close to death, by strictly focusing on the really important things and rejecting anything of lower priority he managed to achieve more than most other people – so much, in fact, that Churchill referred to him as "the Lord of the Heart of the Matter".

In what is reasonably well-documented history, there are only two individuals who have tackled numerous different things – some of them simultaneously – and were successful nonetheless, or at least are considered to have been: Leonardo da Vinci and Johann Wolfgang von Goethe. In both cases there are several indications that they actually dissipated their energies, and that they might have achieved even more and greater things if they had applied some degree of focus. The fact that they left a grand œuvre is clearly owed to their undisputed exceptional gift. But what manager could truthfully claim to come close to Leonardo or Goethe…?

Managerial Compensation

"We will not get the best managers unless we pay the best salaries." This argument, or a variation of it, is commonly used to justify extraordinary managerial income.

Compensation excesses among top U.S. managers dominate the headlines. In Europe we may not pay quite such extraordinary figures yet but, to put it in polite terms, we are making great "advances" in this respect. Asia is the region with the fewest excesses. Until the mid-1990s, "managers' pay" was an important but not necessarily dangerous word – not one that was misused, in any case. Meanwhile it has turned into a public "time bomb".

Are the most expensive managers really the best? Is there a correlation between income levels and leadership qualities? Does the market really put the best people into the best positions?

As long as the stock market boomed and before the scandals were revealed, it may have been justifiable to argue like that, although there had long been reasonable doubt and criticism even before the recent excesses. Now that the scandals have come to light, that argument no longer holds.

There is no doubt that good people must be paid well, even extraordinarily well. The opposite, however, is not true – well-paid people do not necessarily perform well. Why should not cheaper people do a better job than expensive ones?

If some corporations with excessively paid top managers, such as Enron or WorldCom, had been spared these people, not only would they have saved a lot of money but they would probably still exist. No one could have done a worse job managing these companies than the much-vaunted big earners did. A ruined company or a bankruptcy can be had for less.

It is an unproved supposition that a top income will create good performance, let alone top performance. But there are numerous examples of the contrary, enough to take them seriously. No truly great politician has ever gone into politics because of the money. German Chancellors, Swiss Federal Councilors, and American Presidents are relatively poorly paid, yet there have been very capable people among them. The same is true for scientists and top government or military officers. Or take the medical profession, which is often criticized for its high income levels: there are quite a few doctors who do not measure their services in money.

When senior positions automatically come with extra pay, the share of those pushing to the top who are only out for the money is bound to grow. The more of them actually reach the top, the more the organization itself will be money-driven. Money focus, however, is not the same as profit focus. Enron and WorldCom were money-driven but, as everyone knows, they made no profits.

Managerial income and horrendous bonus payments, even in cases of drastic managerial failure, have become a publicy debated question of economic moral and ethics. While the outrage is certainly understandable, it will not produce a solution – for managerial income is not a question of ethics. Also, the frequently demanded regulation at national level is hardly feasible in view of widely varying economic, business, and competitive structures.

But limitations within the individual company are both possible and necessary. Solutions can be found quickly once a ratio between the lowest and the highest salary is set and when managers are paid for future rather than past achievements.

Years ago, Peter F. Drucker reported on a remarkable case. At the beginning of the 20th century, the U.S. tycoon John P. Morgan, one of America's great entrepreneurs and a die-hard capitalist, initiated a study in his widely ramified business empire. He wanted to know where the differences lay between his successful businesses and the less successful ones. It turned out that there was only one point where performers differed from non-performers: It was the difference in salary levels within each company. In successful businesses it was no more than 30 percent from one level to the next; in less successful ones the difference had gotten out of control. J.P. Morgan then introduced the same ratio everywhere.

Today, around 100 years later, we can be a bit more generous with these proportions, especially in case of great achievements, and absolute top performance should be rewarded with a top bonus. But so far I have not found even one financial analyst or headhunter who would have paid attention to that factor in distinguishing performers from non-performers. Perhaps it will be some food for thought to supervisory boards that one of the grandmasters of capitalism, no less, had a clear idea of how compensation should be determined.

Knowledge Management

Lately we have not heard much about one of the New Economy's most colorful buzzwords: knowledge management. That does not mean it has gone out of style. Rather, there are probably not too many managers who have the guts to publicly confess that they are quite clueless (as probably 99 percent of their management colleagues are) or that they question the usefulness of the ideas put forward. Once again, a new playground for IT specialists, consultants and trainers has emerged, enabling them to justify their existence without having to bear the responsibility, cost, or effort associated with it.

I urge managers to remain realistic, and to be careful to check what these emperor's new clothes are really all about. What they will then quickly realize is: not only is the emperor naked – he is not an emperor at all. As so often happens, a combination of false doctrines, bluff, bogus labeling, and showing off prevent the sensible handling of knowledge – one of the key resources of business.

If you just stop to turn off the noise and dig deeper into the matter, you will find out that what is generally referred to as knowledge management is really something else: the management of data, information, and documents. It goes without saying that advances in this field are useful and welcome. It is certainly useful to be able to manage documents, whatever they may be called, better and more transparently, and to make them available more easily to a larger number of people – above all, to the right people – in a wider range of situations. This is achieved with new and better forms of archiving and retrieval, but they are a long shot from being the equivalent of knowledge management.

This is particularly evident on the internet, which, although it contains huge amounts of documents, is definitely not a system of knowledge. Not only does the retrieval problem – the problem of finding what one is looking for – remain unsolved, it is becoming ever more difficult as the internet keeps growing. Even the most powerful search engines are far from finding everything; yet despite this relatively poor performance a typical search will produce tens, even hundreds of thousands of hits. What to do with them? It is not even possible to check them for relevance, let alone obtain true knowledge – in any reasonable sense – of even a fraction of their contents. To talk about managing knowledge in this case is arrant nonsense.

Knowledge is something which, at the present state of things, has nothing to do with computers or IT but with brains, and to an even greater extent with intellect and reason. Knowledge is something that – to put it crudely – has its rightful place between two ears and not between two modems.

The current discussion pays the least attention, if any, to the very sciences and disciplines that have looked most closely at what might deserve to be called knowledge management: these include educational sciences, the psychology of learning and cognition, neurosciences, cybernetics, and certain areas of philosophy. So, in order to strike gold one would have to take one's cue from the results these sciences have produced and develop them further. Instead, and this is typical of so many things that become common practice in management, people naïvely start from scratch – and in most cases that is where they remain, or else they simply change the terminology and speak of knowledge rather than data and information. Nothing is gained by doing that.

How do people change the knowledge they have? Well, they can learn and teach, understand and comprehend, pass on and receive, forget and remember. All of these things have something to do with knowledge. Above all they can think, and that is probably the most important part of knowledge management: thinking things through, perhaps even thinking forward sometimes, and hopefully thinking correctly – in the sense of making logical conclusions. All these are elements of dealing with knowledge. Others that could probably be added are contemplating and discerning, researching, discovering and inventing – and all of them can, perhaps and hopefully, be done far better than they have been done so far.

Of course, we could refer to all of them as "managing" – but what we would gain by doing that is comparable to what we would achieve by referring to cooking as "food management", to the performance of a Beethoven symphony as "sound management", or to the painting of Monet or Cézanne as "brush management".

In other words, it all goes back to a wrong definition of the problem, for knowledge as such cannot be managed. Nobody has realized this more clearly than the man who first recognized the importance of knowledge for modern society, and who coined the terms "knowledge society" and "knowledge worker": Peter F. Drucker. He did not do this in the New Economy context and the IT euphoria, but back in 1969 (!) in his book "The Age of Discontinuity".[18] The term "knowledge management", however, has not appeared in any of Drucker's writings to date – and for good reasons, as he knows all too well that knowledge cannot be managed in any reasonable sense of the word.

What can and must be managed is not knowledge but, in the first place, the work done with knowledge and, secondly, the people doing that work – the knowledge workers. Knowledge, knowledge work and knowledge workers are by no means the same. Only if they are distinguished clearly can management be applied in any reasonable way and produce results.

Knowledge – and this is the consensus view – is the most important resource of a developed economy, and in many industries it has come to be the only one. Anyone succeeding in getting beyond the management of data, information, and documents will have an almost insuperable competitive advantage. To get to that stage, knowledge has to be made productive. There are no magic formulas for that. The only successful way is to manage both knowledge work and knowledge workers – or, to be more precise, brain workers.

Only after this has been understood will we be able to use those forms of communication that really permit the best possible exploitation of existing knowledge. We do not need computers for that, but special structures for interpersonal communication – or, in other words, communication systems. This subject was first investigated around the same time when modern cybernetics emerged, its foundations being laid in the legendary Josiah Macy Conferences in the 1940s, with Alex Bavelas and Heinz von Foerster among the most prominent pioneers.

The point of culmination in cybernetics was reached in the early 1990s when Stafford Beer developed the syntegration method, which is described in his book *Beyond Dispute*. Among other things, it resolved the question of how many people can maximally deal with how many subjects in such a way that all the knowledge available is (mathematically) demonstrably used. It is the most powerful method to date for solving problems in organizations. The targeted use of this method will prove to be an essential factor in the competition for both, creating ever better-performing organizations and handling ever more complexity.

Top Management Teams

As a result of the excesses and scandals at top management level, the word "top management" has been discredited. It is now held at arm's length, metaphorically speaking. This is definitely a dangerous development because there is hardly anything as important as a well-functioning top management team. Even in small companies, and more so in larger ones, the job is usually so complex that the skills of individuals, even highly qualified ones, do not suffice. Top management work almost always is teamwork – which is why the introduction of the CEO principle from the U.S., which was considered a major advance at the time, was in fact a dangerous step backwards.

Contrary to zeitgeist opinion, well-functioning executive top management teams are not characterized by specific emotional dimensions, nor by the much-cited "culture" or by the "chemistry" so often called for. The secret of effective top teams is their adherence to basic principles and rules they have agreed on. When a top management team fails, closer analysis will often reveal that one of the main causes is ignorance of that fact.

Three Basic Principles

The first principle is that the tasks of the executive team must be clear. A team is neither a place for individual or collective self-fulfillment, nor one for democratic consensus discourse – regardless of what some people say. Teams are needed wherever there are tasks to be done which would exceed the strength and abilities of individuals. Otherwise we could spare ourselves the trouble typically associated with teams. It may seem superfluous or trite to demand clarity of tasks, but the truth is that this condition is rarely met.

The second principle is that effective teams need a precise *division of work* because, while their tasks are executed *in a coordinated* fashion, they are not done *jointly* in the narrower sense. Everyone does his or her part of the overall job; the rest need to know what that part is and rely on it being done. This is why good teams have well-thought-out, succinct rules of procedure which clearly define who does what.

The third principle for functional top teams is easy to put in words: it is strict discipline. A lack of it is poisonous for any kind of team, not only in top management, but this is where it does the most harm. Discipline includes the refusal to permit any kind of personality cult or vanity, and it also requires that personal goals be subordinated to those of the company. As long as the two kinds of goals are not in conflict there will be no problems. However, anyone misusing a company – or any other organization – as a vehicle for his or her personal goals constitutes a risk.

Six Rules

In addition to these basic principles, functional teams follow a few basic rules.[14] There are six of them:

First, every member of a top management team has the final say in his sphere of responsibility; there, he speaks on behalf of the whole team and his decisions constitute a commitment for all.

Second, nobody takes a decision in another area of responsibility. These two rules are mutually dependent and complementary. They create clarity and speed and guarantee the group's ability to act. Violations of these two rules will not only create enormous confusion in an organization, thus paralyzing its effectiveness, but in addition they also lead to power struggles.

Third, certain decisions must be left to the team as a whole. This rule provides a safety net against the potential misuse of the first two rules, which, in the absence of a corrective mechanism, could bring about the emergence of "feudal principalities" within an organization, and sooner or later result in the break-up of the team. Speed and the ability to act are important, but they must serve the overriding purpose; therefore certain decisions require everyone's approval. Typical cases include acquisitions or alliances, large-scale innovations, or critical staffing decisions.

Fourth, it is not permitted for team members to make qualifying remarks about each other when outside the team. They do not have to like each other, but there must be no agitation. This rule applies to external behavior only. Within the team there may be fierce debates, which are hard to avoid when it comes to making critical and risky decisions. To the outside, no one is allowed to voice an opinion about team colleagues. No qualifying remarks are permitted, not even praise.

Fifth, each team member is obliged to keep the others informed about what is going on in his area of responsibility. That, too, is a corrective measure for rule No. 1. If there are autonomous decisions in each sphere of responsibility, there must also be comprehensive information to all other team members.

Sixth, contrary to widespread opinion, a well-functioning team is not a group of equals with equal rights, even if the legal system formally requires it. Teams have nothing to do with democracy. What matters is effectiveness. Each individual is a member of the team because he has to make a distinct contribution. That is why functioning teams have an inner structure and a management. The first and most distinguished task of the head of a team in top management – whatever his official title may be – is to ensure that rules are strictly obeyed.

As long as these principles and rules are followed, the often-mentioned "chemistry" among team members is largely meaningless. If the "chemistry" is right, so much the better. If it is not, there will still be a functional team – not by virtue of "chemistry" but because of the rules established. No sensible person would leave an organization to the coincidences of "chemistry".

Coaching

Managers are supposed to enable, empower, support. They are supposed to be coordinators, communicators, cultivators and catalysts, and of course also motivators, moderators, mentors, and mediators. Only one thing is hardly ever heard: that managers are supposed to manage...

High up on the list of role changes supposedly called for in management is coaching. In these days of post-modern linguistic arbitrariness, it is sometimes difficult to tell just what is meant by it. For lack of terminological precision, anyone can make it to mean whatever they want.

The basic idea is quickly clear: according to general understanding, a coach is someone who knows what is good for others – that is to say, for people apparently lacking judgment and decision regarding their own matters. In other words, anyone wishing to make a favorable impression and to be somebody, but unsure how to go about it, needs a personal coach: for his fitness (because he is obviously unable to exercise on his own), for his personality (because he lacks self-confidence), for fashion and style (because he does not dare rely on his own taste), and/ or for his mental and spiritual well-being (because he prefers leading his life by other people's standards rather than taking responsibility for it). Well, everyone is free to do as they please in their private sphere. In the management of organizations, these things are out of place.

Managers' tasks usually have many facets. In most settings, the elements of supervision and advice, of help and support, of moderating and guiding will certainly play a role. There is no doubt that people in organizations occasionally need these dimensions of leadership in order to perform, cope with difficulties, and get over setbacks.

None of those things, however, is essential to the managerial function. What managers have to do in the first place is manage. Their primary task is to produce results, thus accomplishing the purpose of their company. That is the sole reason why they are needed, and that is what they are paid for. To this end, they have to make use of their people's strengths, in order to enable them to deliver a performance for the company.

The job of management is not to change people, nor is it to eliminate their weaknesses, but to transform strengths into results.

Management is the profession of effectiveness. It is not cleverness, intelligence, experience, emotion, vision, or talent that counts, but what you achieve with them and what you make of them. Management is about the execution of clearly defined tasks; they are determined by discipline, performance, and responsibility.

As a concession to zeitgeist preferences, this might also be called coaching. However, nothing is gained by doing so; in fact, it leads to a confusion of terms and to deceptive labeling. Even worse, it deprives coaching of its value where coaching is truly called for: in the specific individual case. Coaching must never be considered as a general substitute for management.

Outside the company and in private life, it is perfectly fine to take a different view. There, management may be superfluous and even a nuisance.

In companies, however, and in other institutions of society that have to achieve results, management is the indispensable shaping and actuating agent. All this may be considered unimportant when times are good, when businesses run themselves and when there are no major problems. Such conditions, however, are not typical in business and industry, nor are they any measure of the quality of management. Management needs to prove itself under heavy weather conditions; it has to be designed to meet the demands that will be made upon it in the most difficult, the hardest of cases. As long as everything goes smoothly there is no need for managers – moderators, custodians, coordinators and coaches will do. There is a reason why phenomena like these emerge in good times, as a result of a sustained increase in prosperity – quite pleasant, but actually a luxury that people enjoy as long as they can afford it.

Innovation

The fact that innovation is important hardly needs stressing. The future of virtually every company depends on it. However, it cannot be repeated often enough that most attempts at innovation fail. Eight out of ten innovations come to grief – and the costs are appalling.

The main reason is that, although in most companies innovation has a lot of romantic appeal to it there is usually only little professionalism in dealing with it. The majority of managers are not masters of the craft. Every innovation is an "expedition into uncharted territory", a "first ascent", but most of them are treated as if they were a Sunday afternoon walk in the park.

We need to begin by abandoning some widely held false doctrines and misconceptions.

The first is that innovations originate in research laboratories or R&D departments. What originates there are not innovations but ideas, perhaps even prototypes or experimental results. Innovation has to be defined completely and absolutely from the vantage point of the market.

Only after marketing successes have begun to materialize can managers permit themselves and their staff to speak of innovation. Only by looking at things in this light is it possible to choose the correct strategies and arrive at a fairly reasonable estimate of the time and money required. The essential question is not: "What have we developed, invented or discovered that is new?" The key question is: "What do we need and what do we have to do to successfully launch this development, invention or discovery in the market?"

The second false doctrine is that creativity is key. As a consequence, it is demanded of managers as one of their salient attributes; creativity workshops are conducted and creativity tools applied. Apparently, people believe that there is a shortage of ideas. However, it is not ideas that are lacking but ideas that are put into practice. Even in the most "uncreative" of companies there is a vastly greater number of ideas than will ever get implemented.

Generating ideas is something entirely different from implementing them. And without implementation there is no innovation. Ideas are not unimportant, of course, but they are the least important, the cheapest and the simplest of all elements. After an idea has been generated, a functional prototype has to be developed or clinical tests carried out. That alone involves much more effort and expense, and it takes far longer. After that, the development has to be brought to maturity – once again at considerably higher cost in terms of time and money. And finally, at least the marketing phase has to be launched. It is safe to assume that each successive step involves ten times more effort and expense than the previous one.

The third wrong belief is that only small companies are innovative. It is fashionable these days to criticize the unwieldiness of large companies and to praise the virtues of small ones. There are lots of things that small companies can do and big ones cannot, but innovating is not one of them. Small units are often more creative, they find it easier to generate ideas and they quickly get to the prototype phase. At that point, however, most of them are on the ropes.

Small companies usually have two problems: they are underfinanced and undermanaged. That is why many small, supposedly innovative companies are in fact no more than attractive takeover candidates for big companies. Small companies are good sprinters but poor finishers. Effective innovation, however, is a long-distance run, a discipline that requires endurance, where it is crucial to save enough strength for the second half.

A fourth misbelief is that innovation is always or preferably about high tech. The general fascination with and fixation on technology has resulted in a collective delusion. We will certainly have some more high technology in the future, and there certainly are companies that need to concern themselves with that issue – some, mind you, not all. Owing to the excessive fascination with it, people tend to overlook the fact that the low-tech and no-tech fields offer far more opportunities for lucrative business involving less risk and less expense.

The fifth and most dangerous error, however, is the view that a special type of personality is needed to innovate: the proactive, creative, entrepreneurial, venturesome pioneer. Such people do exist but they are rare. A closer look at the supposed pioneers will almost always reveal that they were put on this pedestal in retrospect by hero-worshipping biographies or media reports.

Most pioneers were in fact perfectly ordinary people. Before their success became obvious, they were often regarded as eccentrics or freaks by those around them. There was nothing of the "glamorous innovator" about them. Yet there is one thing most of them did have: a systematic approach. They mastered their craft. Though it is hardly ever mentioned in their biographies, that is what we can learn from them.

Culture

Let me give you the essence right up front: bad management is driven by culture – good management usually is not.

The notion that the kind of management a person practices depends on certain aspects of culture may seem obvious and plausible, but as virtually everywhere in management, plausibility once again is a bad advisor. The idea of culture driving everything, resulting in a need for inter- and multicultural management, is a half-truth at best.

There is a host of publications dealing with the topic of "culture-boundness", related training programs are in ample supply and, as always happens with management methods, they are thrown on the market rapidly. The sheer speed at which some people – whose views on the subject were never heard before – now present themselves as experts is enough to warrant skepticism.

The widespread but often remarkably superficial preoccupation with corporate culture has given rise to false doctrines that are harmful to management in practice, an unfortunate development further exacerbated by the discussion about globalization.

The basic problem is that people fail to make a few important distinctions. Firstly, they do not distinguish between good and bad management. Secondly, they do not differentiate between the "what" and the "how" of management. Thirdly, they draw the wrong conclusions regarding an organization's management based on the geographical location it operates in.

When distinguishing good management from bad, this is what you will quickly realize:

The *what* of good management is largely the same for all cultures. What professional managers do hardly differs across regions. The reason is simple: what needs to be done is exclusively determined by the requirements of a well-functioning organization. That is why these managers are effective – no matter what culture they come from.

How things are done can differ greatly, and usually does. Among other things, the way in which tasks are performed and in which people behave depends on their culture, but in the case of managers this is not the only decisive factor. Factors of at least equal importance are the individual company's industry and line of business or a region's specific demographic and social conditions, such as the population's average level of education.

For instance, in any well-managed organization (but not in poorly managed ones) you will find clear targets and effective control, irrespective of whether you are dealing with an Italian, Spanish, or Chinese organization. The way those targets are defined and monitored may differ from one culture to another. Also, good organizations will usually have effective meetings, elaborate communication systems, efficient work, performance qualification, and the systematic promotion of young talent. In short: there are many different ways of doing things – but for identical purposes.

The same applies if culture is not defined by ethnicity or nationality, as in the previous example, but by other criteria:

whether an organization is knowledge-based or labor-intensive, whether it belongs to the world of fashion or technology, whether it produces investment or consumer goods – the "what" of good management is the same, the "how" can vary.

Differences are owed not so much to culture but to the specific requirements of industries, products, and customers. Hence, the concept of culture should not – as is often the case – be simply related to national or ethnic idiosyncrasies. As we can see, there are more and additional dimensions.

Wrong Insights – Misleading Solution Concepts

The insufficient distinction between the "what" and the "how" of management leads many to demand different – culture-bound – kinds of management. These attempted explanations do nothing to enhance people's understanding; indeed, they only add to the confusion.

In some cases, differences are exaggerated to an unnecessary degree; in others, outer appearances are confused with substance due to a lack of observation and true knowledge about management.

Typical examples include the exorbitant exaggerations when referring to Japanese management from the mid-1980s until roughly the mid-1990s. Later on, when Japan's crisis became undeniably clear, a few things that true connoisseurs of Japan had known all along became obvious to the world: first, that Japanese management is by no means superior to Western management by virtue of culture – and thus by nature – as had often been claimed, and second, that Japanese organizations which operate successfully for a sustained period of time are usually managed by standards very similar to those applied in other regions of the world.

There is no reason to fuss about inter- and multicultural management. It goes without saying that every country has its own customs and traditions, which anyone traveling there ought to know and respect as a matter of basic courtesy. This has little to do with management. A minimum of manners, decency, and breeding, resulting from an education that deserves the name, should be expected of employees and executives. And while I will readily admit that these things can no longer be taken for granted nowadays – probably due, above all, to the rapidly increasing number of managers a modern society needs – it seems very wrong to me to speak of different kinds of management, simply because there are people with educational deficits even in senior positions.

A similarly misleading view has emerged with regard to "international" management. In fact, a closer look reveals that there has never been a thing of the sort – nor its opposite, which would be national management. What does exist and has always existed are different business profiles in terms of geography; that is, companies operating at the national or international level. In the latter case it is obviously indispensable to have adequate knowledge of languages, customs and traditions, and local conditions. But once again, that does not have anything to do with management as such, but with the specific context in which it takes place. It has to do with the field of application of management.

Management is right or wrong, good or bad, capable or incapable. It is not national or international, mono- or multicultural.

It depends as little on the nation or culture as a sport properly practiced.

The Logic of Progress

The crucial point is that there are always many more ways of doing things wrong than of doing them right. Wrong management has numerous manifestations because everyone has his own way of acting wrongly. Right management, however, has limited variations.

This is another point of analogy with sports: golf – if done correctly – is played the same way everywhere, as is tennis or chess. There are many ways to play golf wrongly, but only one way of doing it right. Similarly, the rules of effectiveness and professionalism for managers are the same everywhere – just like linguistic rules, to use another example. English, spoken correctly, is the same all over the world because there is only one way to speak it properly and well. The proof is in the very fact that English, worldwide, is spoken with incorrect grammar, bad style, and poor pronunciation with the exception of a certain educated stratum. That, however, would never cause an anglicist to call it inter- or multicultural; the same is true for golf pros and their sport.

The conclusion from all this concerns both economics and time: There is no need for employees to be trained in different kinds of management. One kind is enough: right and good management. Not only will this approach save time and costs; it will also lead to a marked improvement in professionalism because all the aberrations are avoided.

The different fields of application of right management may then require additional skills, such as language skills, a knowledge of regional history or of local customs and traditions. The basis for that, however, is the kind of management know-how acquired and continually perfected through good education – an education focusing on the key factors of professionalism, rather than on dubious views rooted in superficialities and often in a lack of expertise.

Customer

The danger associated with the word "customer" is that it can easily be underestimated, which means that those concerned lose sight of the key element of a business enterprise, of its very purpose. If anyone had told me at the beginning of the 1990s I would have listened in disbelief – but that is exactly what happened under the influence of the shareholder value principle. It was the main reason for numerous balance sheet scandals and bankruptcies, for the financial distress of many companies and their need for a turnaround, which became obvious when the stock markets started crashing in March 2000.

With increasing popularity of the shareholder value concept, it became legitimate to focus on shareholder interests only and, de facto, turn away from the customer and from customer value. That, in turn, enabled a certain type of person to ascend to top positions: I am talking about the type of manager for whom quantifiable things – or, even worse: those quantifiable in cash – are the only kind that matter. The result was an epoch of abbreviated and one-dimensional corporate management.

All the progress previously made in corporate management theory could now be ignored. At that point it had become very clear that companies must be perceived as complex, multi-dimensional systems and that management is the art of balancing numerous, often conflicting factors – insights that people now thought could be disregarded. All of a sudden, corporate management had become easy: simple indicators of its effectiveness were the daily stock market prices, which (an apparent law of nature to the historically illiterate) were rising continually and without bounds.

Another thing that was thrown to the winds was a key insight from strategy theory, according to which a successful strategy must be aimed at serving markets – which in a market economy is synonymous with customers – more successfully than competitors can. Now, the term strategy was understood to mean making deals and satisfying the expectations of the stock market crowd – of analysts and the media.

Up until then, no one but Marxists and communists had denied shareholders' well-defined interests and their being entitled to capital returns and growth. It had been equally clear, however, that these aims could only be achieved one way: by focusing management's attention on the true purpose of a company – customer satisfaction.

Doing business is a complex thing, but its underlying logic is simple: a company with customers will always have access to capital – whether from the stock market or from other sources. Conversely, the New Markets have clearly shown that a company can have all the capital it wants – if it fails to find customers it will soon be out of business. The fact that an idea is able to attract stock market capital is no indication of its suitability for customers. And it is the customers, not the shareholders, who ultimately pay the bill. In a figurative sense, shareholders pay "the bill" only when the company has failed to fulfill its main mission: finding customers, attracting and satisfying them. Cus-

tomer orientation is aimed at the creation of economic output –
shareholder orientation is aimed at its distribution. The former
is the difficult part, the latter is easy.

Growth

After "profit", the second most popular term in management is "growth". It is a dangerous word, as long as no distinction is made between growth that is right and growth that is wrong, and between healthy and unhealthy growth.

Most corporate strategies in the boom of the 1990s were radically wrong. There is no glossing over this fact. The strategies so impressively presented by consultants and managers were roads to disaster. The consequences were retreats on all fronts, capacity cutbacks, dismissals, balance sheet falsifications, frauds and excessive enrichment at the expense of companies and shareholders, and in many cases the threat of insolvency.

Even though the debacle has been taking place in front of everyone's eyes, it is yet to affect the thinking of many managers – including those who, as successors to the ones that failed, are confronted with the smoking ruins every day. They continue to operate with the same wrong categories. When asked what their most important strategic goals are, their reflexive answer is: profit and growth.

Growth, although unquestionably an important factor in entrepreneurial endeavor, is wrong and dangerous as a strategic target. It will inevitably take a company down the road to failure. Growth cannot be an input to a strategy, it is its output. It must not be set as a goal to start with; it is the outcome of thoroughly thinking about the business and its intrinsic laws. Until these facts are firmly fixed in the minds of managers and supervisory bodies, there will only be temporary improvements and people will keep on making the same mistakes.

Real expertise in strategic planning is demonstrated only when a distinction is made between healthy and unhealthy growth. If a twelve-year-old grows a few inches every year he is healthy; if a fifty-year-old does the same there is something seriously wrong with him. Size as such can never be a strategic goal. A company does not need to be big, it needs to be strong. There is no conceivable set of circumstances in which the size of a company is of strategic importance. Anyone focusing on size is allowing himself to be fooled by an optical illusion and, metaphorically speaking, unable to tell muscle from fat. People are led astray by the fact that while correct strategies almost always produce growth and ultimately size, the reverse is not true. Size can also result from wrong strategies.

Size is measured by sales revenues or, nowadays less frequently, by headcount. As the recent past has shown, sales revenues can be increased relatively quickly and easily if it is done in the wrong way: through inconsiderate geographical expansion or product range enlargement, or wrong acquisitions and mergers. Inevitable consequences are an increase in complexity and a decline in earning power. The absolute figures, however, go up, and since they are clearly visible they are considered to be proof of success. The ratios deteriorate – but because they are either invisible or concealed they go unnoticed.

There are only two measurable parameters that can be used to reliably distinguish healthy from unhealthy growth.

The first is market position: Size and growth are only healthy when they result from an improvement in market position. (Note that the reverse is not true: growth and size alone do not necessarily strengthen the market position.)

The second and far more important yardstick is productivity. Only the best companies have a dedicated set of tools to measure it. Productivity is still neglected, wrongly defined, and wrongly measured in most cases. When defined as "total factor productivity", it is the one and only reliable indicator by which to judge growth.

Only if total factor productivity grows along with sales revenues can we speak of healthy growth – growth that produces muscular power and strength, to remain within the medical metaphor. If total factor productivity stagnates while a company grows, that company is headed towards obesity. This may be something one can live with – to a certain degree. If, however, total factor productivity declines when there is growth, the company is suffering from cancer. Tumors grow quickly, and in the end the patient dies. Only in its very early stages can this disorder be treated – and only in some cases.

Economic Errors

Shareholder

Massive misunderstandings about doing business have led to much confusion. The Wall Street industry's promotion machinery "invented" the investor and made the world believe it was the same as an entrepreneur – more even: the prototype of the new, modern entrepreneur. What years ago would have been referred to as an investor or, much more frequently, a stock speculator, is now supposed to be the measure of entrepreneurial action. That is one of the main causes of both the unfortunate economic development during the 1990s and the current crisis.

One thing is certain: every entrepreneur is an investor. But is the opposite equally true – is every investor an entrepreneur? Due to the development on the stock exchanges and in the money markets, an important distinction in the public perception is becoming increasingly blurred: the distinction between the investor shareholder and the entrepreneurial shareholder. While it is a fact that ownership in a company and ownership of shares is certified by the same document, and perhaps there is not even a legal difference between the two, there is a world of difference both economically and socially.

The creators of the concept believe they have invented a new form of capitalism. Some complain about it, but the majority welcomes it. Whatever one may personally think of it – the fact is that only half of the truth has been considered so far, and only this half has been important. Lately we have been forced to acknowledge the second half as well (as the Japanese have for quite a while). There is an old wisdom among the big capitalists of all times: "If you can't sell you have to care." An investor operates temporarily; he is only interested in his securities as long as they yield returns. Entrepreneurial activity, however, is designed to stretch over the long term.

An investor-shareholder will give up as soon as problems materialize: he will sell. And if he is smart he will place his investments in such a way that he can get out quickly; for instance, by investing in highly liquid markets where even large volumes can be sold off easily. An entrepreneur-shareholder responds to problems very differently: He struggles ... he "cares". Why he struggles does not really matter – what matters is that he does.

Some may struggle simply because they are unable to sell. To others their enterprise may be more than just a cash machine – it may be their life's work, even that of generations before them. Others may struggle because they are wildly determined never to return into dependent employment. Whatever it may be in the individual case – the entrepreneur-shareholder struggles, not because he is a hero but because he has no choice. His alternative would be financial ruin.

The investor is interested in one resource only: in money. It is what he strives to maximize. By contrast, the task of an entrepreneur must inevitably be focused on several resources. It is, in fact, defined by combining resources which need to be balanced as creatively and productively as possible.

The investor-shareholder is only interested in financial returns. There is no need for him to care about anything else except, perhaps, when it helps him decide what shares to buy. The entrepreneur-shareholder cares about financial returns, too; beyond that, however, he also cares about the performance and strength of the entire company, that is to say, about all factors relevant to performance – even if it is not always convenient or easy for him. He simply has no choice.

For an investor, the stock exchange is indispensable. If it did not exist he could not pursue his investment goals, much less accomplish them. He would have to become an entrepreneur. The entrepreneur, on the other hand, does not need the stock exchange. Entrepreneurs also exist in the absence of stock markets – as important as the latter may be in many respects. There were entrepreneurs long before there were stock markets, even before there were banks; they also existed when stock markets and banks broke down and had to be closed temporarily. Contrary to widespread opinion, the stock market is not only a system for raising capital but in many cases a system of capital destruction. In actual fact, it is a system of capital valuation, which does not mean that it values correctly.

Investors – in particular those of the shareholder-value variety – are only found in bull markets. Only there can they disseminate the illusion of creating values. In a bear market, everything is reversed: Investors destroy value and capital – and they do so actively – because the only way for them to achieve returns is by going short. The more the stock prices plunge, the more delighted they will be with naked sales and put options. Entrepreneurs, by contrast, are economic all-weather types. They must be able to work independently of stock markets. They create value especially when prices are lowest and no investor is interested in buying.

Stakeholder

Two key concepts of the 1990s, shareholder and shareholder value, have lost much of their appeal in recent years. The suspicion is slowly spreading that it could have been precisely these concepts and the corporate management, assessment and valuation based on them that led to the various bubbles and their disastrous consequences.

Instead of everyone pausing for thought and rethinking the matter thoroughly, the next misleading idea has promptly been introduced; instead of shareholders we now have stakeholders.

It is true, its proponents argue, that a company should not solely be managed in the interest of a single constituency, the shareholders; instead, *several* interest groups must be considered – that is to say, all stakeholders. Several dangerous errors are associated with that word.

Stakeholder Orientation Leads to Poor Corporate Management

By no means does the term "stakeholder" lead to a truly effective reform of shareholder value thinking. On the contrary, it causes even more serious errors in corporate management than shareholder orientation does.

In historical terms, the stakeholder approach was the precursor of the shareholder concept. In 1952, Ralph Cordiner, then CEO of General Electric, used the term when replying to the question: *"Whom does the top management of a public company respond to?"*

Correct and important as the question may have been, Cordiner's answer was wrong. The stakeholder approach failed, and this was what ultimately led to the development of the supposedly superior shareholder approach. Its inventor, Alfred Rappaport, believed it could be used to make lazy managers get into gear.

He wanted to keep them from justifying low returns on the grounds of having to consider the interests of all stakeholders, rather than just those of a single group – the shareholders. Rappaport and others correctly and clearly recognized that a management body that was (or pretended to be) accountable to all interest groups, and therefore wanted or had to please them all, in fact no longer had any responsibility. It was always possible to excuse one's actions by saying that one interest or another had to be satisfied – whatever seemed most convenient at the moment. One day it was the interest of employees and unions, another day it was the concerns of suppliers, the general public, of scientists, politicians, and so forth. In short, poor corporate performance always had a "good reason". Not that the stakeholder approach made good management performance impossible. There were excellently managed firms at the time; General Electric is one of the names that come to mind. Still, the stakeholder approach enabled bad managers to evade responsibility whenever they pleased, simply by giving plausible and, in the context of that approach, undisputable reasons.

Any theory of corporate management that centers around interest groups – regardless of how they are defined and how many there are – will inevitably put the company at the mercy of the changing balance of power amongst those interest groups. As a result, there can no longer be any useful measures of management performance. The consequences are devastating, as is confirmed by historical examples. Just think of the British industrial sector and the stranglehold the trade unions had on it for three decades after World War II, and how it almost perished in the process; or of the companies trapped in the mire of political corruption in Italy during that time, or of the collapse of nationalized industries in Austria during the 1970s and 1980s.

Rappaport's supposed improvement was in fact a "disimprovement", as the excesses and debacles of the 1990s clearly show. There is only one way of managing a company well: the enterprise itself must be the center of attention. This means that management has to take its bearings from the company's own performance and competitiveness: they provide sufficiently clear measures by which the actions of top management are to be guided and assessed.

What is good for a company may not be equally good for all interest groups, but it satisfies the largest possible number of legitimate interests. In the final analysis, low-performing companies cannot satisfy any of the interests involved.

Job Security Is Not a Corporate Purpose

Arguing against shareholder and stakeholder value does not imply a relapse into welfare state thinking, as some people claim, nor does it come with a bias for job creation. While it is true that, depending on the political situation, one can usually gather brownie points by calling for more employment – something that politicians, but also entrepreneurs, top managers, and union officials are susceptible to doing – it is definitely not a solution. This becomes very evident when the focus is on the individual company and its ability to function and perform.

The task of a company is to provide an economic service for the market – or, in other words: a service for customers. The company fulfils its obligation in society by creating satisfied customers. If a large number of employees are needed to do this, it may make the unions happy. If, however, the company is able to carry out its task with fewer and fewer employees it should not be prevented from cutting jobs. Customer satisfaction must always have priority over the interests of employees.

Customers Are Not Stakeholders

The emphasis on the customer immediately causes supporters of the stakeholder approach to claim that the customer is a stakeholder, too.

That is a serious error in terms of the logic of business and corporate management. Customers are not an interest group because they have no interest in the company. Regardless of how important a supplier may be, the customer is fundamentally indifferent to the company he buys from because he has a choice. In fact, this choice is what defines the term "customer" in a market economy. If a customer is not satisfied with one company's products or services he can always turn to another. Hence it is unrealistic to expect loyalty from customers, although every attempt should be made to achieve it. What appears to be loyalty is, in fact, always the result of a benefit analysis. The customer pays for the benefit he receives.

At this point a frequent objection is that the customer has an interest in the continued existence of a company because he needs a supplier and often depends on that supplier. Well, there is no doubt the customer needs a supplier, but in a functioning market economy there will always be several ways of procuring what is needed. Every customer has a vital interest in *not* becoming dependent on one supplier because otherwise, as a result of his lack of a choice, he would cease to be a customer and become dependent on a monopoly. However close and good – even friendly – the relationship between a customer and a supplier may be, it is always based on the customer's satisfaction, which is linked to his benefit and his ability to choose.

There is only one sound rationale for good corporate management: providing the customer with better service than existing competitors can. In other words, customer benefit and competitiveness are the two unerring and non-manipulable guiding principles for corporate management.

Inflation and Deflation

As governments and central banks perceive the current crisis to be a financial crisis in essence, vast amounts are spent to save banks and boost the economy – so much, in fact, that according to conventional economic theory we are facing a case of racing inflation.

This is what mainstream economists proclaim, and it is what the media propagate. As a result, most people – in particular corporate decision-makers – firmly believe that current measures to fight the crisis will cause a sharp inflation and thus currency devaluation.

But what if the funds made available never actually reach the economy? For instance, six months after the crisis-triggering collapse of Lehman Brothers, we observed that of the nearly 1000 billion dollars in bank rescue funds made available by the U.S. government, only 5 percent had actually found their way into the economy. In Germany, less than 2 percent did. If these funds are not to be captured by consumers and businesses, inflation is very unlikely to happen. So will there be deflation instead?

What Is Inflation?

There is an almost universal reflex to worry about inflation when prices increase. It is true that inflation has something to do with rising prices and, to the same extent, with a devaluation of purchasing power. But price increases are not always inflationary. When, for instance, the oil price quintuples within just a few weeks, this has nothing to do with inflation, nor does it warrant any forecasts to that effect.

When and why do prices go up? They go up when demand exceeds supply. And when they do, there will usually be a decline in demand – due to the very fact that prices increase – or an increase in supply. As a result, prices go back to normal. This, precisely, is one of the effects of efficient markets. It is part and parcel of the ups and downs of doing business. So there can be no inflation as a result.

What many people obviously do not know is that inflation can occur *only* if demand does not decline, despite increasing prices. This happens when prices are kept artificially high, thus overriding market mechanisms; for instance, due to wage increases enforced by labor unions, or because salaries and pensions are tied to the price index.

What Is Deflation?

Deflation is the general decrease of prices which have previously undergone inflationary increase, in particular the material prizes such as securities, real estate, commodities, and precious metals. Why does deflation occur? The main cause of deflation is debtors' inability to settle the loans they have previously taken out to buy these high-priced goods. If they had not obtained any loans they would not have been able to buy the goods, hence the prices would not have risen excessively.

When the prices of credit-financed material assets decrease, the bank's right to subsequent collateral will be applied: the borrower will be required to provide additional collateral when the credit sum still outstanding is no longer covered by the value of the asset collateralized.

If, however, the debtor is unable to provide additional collateral he will have to reduce his debt. To do so, he will have to raise cash, which he can do from any reserves he may have. In the absence of reserves he will have to sell something in order to raise cash.

So the inflation in asset prices due to excessive credit financing is followed by a general pressure to sell assets, as debtors need to raise liquid funds to service distressed loans. The need to raise cash leads to forced sales, at any price, which further drives the decline of material asset prices. A vicious circle has been set in motion. The downward spiral is turning.

So the question is, are we heading towards deflation? No. We are not headed towards it – it is in full swing. And it will last until the general debt problem is finally solved, either by settling the debt or by eliminating it otherwise.

You can lead a horse to the water but you can't make him drink, or so the saying goes. Another one says you cannot push a waggon with a rope. Or in other words: no matter how much money is pumped into the economy – under circumstances like these, it will fail to boost the economy, and thus will not cause inflation. The deflation situation simply cannot be explained with conventional theories.

U.S. Management Superiority

It is time to stop imitating American management fashions, in particular in corporate governance. Instead, we ought to remember our tried and tested capabilities and strengths and return to a sensible way of doing business.

Two misconceptions have led to the naïve imitation of the seemingly superior U.S. approaches to management. The first misconception is that the American economy is strong. In fact, it is only big. The second is that this supposed strength is owed to the good, globally superior management of U.S. companies. The fact is that the American approach to management is only useful in a relatively simple setting. For complex, multicultural, or even global tasks it is unsuitable and downright harmful.

The U.S. economy is in a desperate state which is being concealed by incorrect figures, biased reporting and dubious economic theory. The growth rates given for the national product are not correct, nor are the employment figures or company profits reported; indeed there has not been an economic recovery worth mentioning since the recession of 2000 through 2002. In hindsight, the economic theory of the "asset-based, wealth-driven economy" which is prevalent in the U.S. is turning out to be just another bad joke of economic history.

The size of American companies is not owed to the quality of their management. The U.S. economy is big because it has something no other developed country has ever had: a big and largely homogeneous home market. It comes as no surprise that big companies can sprout and grow in an economy with 290 million or so consumers, all speaking the same language, and with a mentality that makes them susceptible to consistent advertising and promotion and which facilitates uniform product design.

Management is easy when there are no customs frontiers to be overcome and the same rules of administration and tax laws apply everywhere. None of these things existed in Europe until recently. We can be envious of that comfortable position but we should not try to copy the American way of doing things.

The export rate of the typical U.S. company is small to non-existent, that of a typical European company is high. America is an importing nation, Europe lives on exports. Wherever English is not spoken, the American way of management is soon at the end of its wits. For these reasons, and contrary to what many believe, the United States is far from being the center of global thinking and global business. If anything, its center is where business relations with China and Japan existed as far back as over 500 years ago, and where there is no need to fuss over ideas of globalization because they have long been implemented: in Europe.

For all these reasons, it is much easier to manage a big company in the U.S. than it is in Europe. There is no reason to look to America in hopes of learning how to manage under complex conditions. If American management is the standard program – managing a big company in Europe is the "freestyle" version.

Americanized and MBA-trained managers will quickly realize that managing a company is not about solving case studies but the exact opposite: it is about recognizing where what "case" might be looming. Once everything can be laid down neatly in a case study, that case is no longer a problem but just a piece of work to be done. When you can get ready to draw up a business plan, just like you have learned in business school, others have long closed the deal because they responded to faint signals instead of waiting for the numbers. Business administration is exactly what the name says: administration – not anticipatory, entrepreneurial, or even strategic action.

This generation will learn from first-hand experience that what have been propagated all over the world as the ultimate truths and factors of orientation – shareholders, stakeholders, and value creation – are, in fact, the exact opposite: factors of disorientation. Hence, confusion and disorientation are already beginning to show in the higher echelons of management – more and more difficult to conceal, though still covered up with braggadocio.

EBIT, EBITDA

Quite a percentage of managers seem to believe that knowledge of key financial indicators is evidence of management competence. A dangerous error.

As long as EBIT the only to measure of company performance, the risk of faulty management was limited. Yet even that key indicator was misused.

At *Malik Management*, we have been working with EBIT in strategy consulting at least since 1984. It was not as new as many people believed when it became fashionable in the mid-1990s.

However, before the start of the bubble years, EBIT was never used or recommended for the management of a company. Its purpose was to compare businesses. Since every business is in a different financial and tax situation, it was necessary to use gross rather than net results in order to be able to make sensible performance comparisons.

The cradle of EBIT was the so-called PIMS (Profit Impact of Market Strategies) program, which was developed by General Electric during the 1960s to assess and compare the performance of different business units. It was, of course, always understood that genuine results could only be those after interest and tax and that dividends could only come into the equation beyond that point.

Under the influence of the shareholder value concept, what had been invented for the purpose of comparison then became a management measure. It was the first step towards wrong management.

The next steps were predetermined and inevitable. EBITD, EBITDA, etc. were invented – all of them key indicators from the world of accountants, auditors, and investment bankers, and all of them completely useless for the purpose of managing a company. At a symposium I once took the liberty to suggest a "completely new" indicator: EBA – *Earnings Before Anything*. The audience took a while to get the irony.

These financial indicators may be valuable in various cases. They are, however, of little use for the management of a company – the very function that has to produce the economic result before it can be assigned a value.

All financial indicators are highly problematic for management because they follow on the truly important developments with a time lag. Of the broad range of indicators that have emerged over time, only one is really suitable for management purposes: EAE – *Earnings After Everything*. Only after all the necessary provisions have been made, and all reserves have been set up to allow the company to get through hard times, can we talk of genuine results.

Stock Options

After the recent excesses, the dangers of the term "stock options" hardly need to be pointed out. It is about time to stop trying to repair systems that have never worked and never will. As Peter F. Drucker said several decades ago, "There are no good executive compensation plans. There are only bad and worse."

Probably no one has seen more "ingeniously conceived, brilliantly designed, and carefully calculated" compensation systems fail than Drucker has. They regularly came up in boom phases and, when those phases ended, collapsed with equal regularity. If any more evidence was ever needed to substantiate this observation, it was provided in the 1990s. Now is the time for a new start, and it is a good opportunity, too – in the very interest of the top managers currently under fire.

Even the most sophisticated reforms currently undertaken to save or conceal the ruins of stock option programs and the like will not solve the problem. There is no arithmetic-mechanical system that could effectively determine *the* right compensation for the complex tasks of top management. No such system would come to grips with the rapid change of conditions under which it is supposed to function. The inventors of these systems have not even taken into consideration most of these conditions.

No arithmetic system will work for rising and falling stock prices alike, during boom phases and recessions, for business-as-usual and for turnaround cases, for acquisitions and divestitures. There is no system that, by using mechanical calculation, could take proper account of even the most essential dimensions of corporate management – operative and strategic, short and long term, today and tomorrow.

What is the alternative? It is an autonomous decision by the supervisory body, taking into account all relevant circumstances without restraint. This solution is far from being ideal but it is the best, once people have understood that the ideal is a mere illusion and, as such, not feasible.

It enables the supervisory body to win back its most important function, which it has been ceding to rigid mechanics: to determine and evaluate the company's overall performance, how it was achieved, and what each executives contributed to it. This is clearly one of the most difficult tasks in the context of management and control, but it is also the most important and noble one. It represents the key purpose of the supervisory body, the very source of its true significance. There will be no effective corporate governance unless this task is performed competently and responsibly.

The implications are unpleasant but beneficial to the function of the company and indispensable for its health. With compensations determined in this way, top managers will no longer be able to simply derive their own performance from the relations between a set of monetary figures which they can easily manipulate. Rather, they will have to present their achievements convincingly, provide solid evidence, and point out causes and influences. The supervisory body, in turn, will have to deal with the overall situation of the company and its management thoroughly enough to be able to execute its task competently. That requires some work – but after all, this is what the supervisory body is appointed and paid to do. In companies with sophisticated management systems it has always been that way.

The main counter-arguments are easy to invalidate. One is that the supervisory body cannot do all these things because its members are too far removed from day-to-day reality. Well, wherever that is the case they will just have to move closer. Another argument is that the supervisory body does not have the competencies. In that case it will be about time to staff it with competent people. A third argument is that managers would then make less money. Now that depends on the supervisory body – it could also be more. Some say the decisions will be subjective. That is correct but irrelevant. Every court decision is subjective because it is taken by a thinking, considering, judging individual or group of people. The important point is that decisions must not be arbitrary, and we know from 200 years' experience with constitutional states that this can be ensured. Finally, one counter-argument goes like this: managers would not know in advance earned how much they will make in the course of the year. That is right and a good thing, too. It is precisely the situation that entrepreneurs face: they never know their income in advance.

U.S. Economic Miracle

It is remarkable with what naïveté and blindness American management ideas have been adopted in Europe over the past few years. As mentioned before, the argument was the same every time: Since U.S. companies are so successful, U.S. management must be good. So let us manage the American way and our economy will prosper. This was like opening the gates to a Trojan horse.

Anyone skeptical enough to take a closer look at the issue soon came to the conclusion that the much-praised and naïvely admired American economic miracle never happened. It was a media event, nothing else.

Even the developments leading up to the housing bubble were celebrated as a sign of American economic prowess. Higher and higher loans for less and less solvent buyers of dodgier and dodgier houses were believed to be signs of particularly visionary business activities. European business practices seemed backward and incompetent by comparison. One of the silliest economic theories invented by U.S. economists to legitimize real-estate financing, the 'asset wealth theory', was believed to be particularly progressive. This way the ground was prepared, with much public acclaim, for one of history's greatest financial debacles.

First, even in their official version, American growth rates are no higher now than they were in earlier periods, as a comparison spanning the time since World War II reveals. In addition, two effects artificially increased them: the financial bubble and – even more so – the statistical impact of what is generally referred to as "hedonic price indexing". No one else calculates like this, yet everybody marveled at the U.S. growth rates.

Second, there has never been a productivity miracle, except in the small computer manufacturing niche. Professor Robert Gordon of Chicago's Northwestern University, one of the few clear-sighted analysts of the productivity figures published, showed that there has never been any quantitative evidence of the alleged increases in productivity. Only certain consulting companies, which also erred tremendously on other matters, believe in the fairy tale of the particularly repid rise in productivity in the American economy.

Third, U.S. profits were not the result of genuine economic performance but of creative accounting – which in the end came down to balance sheet fraud. That is also why they are now collapsing. They resulted from four things: one, wrong book entries on stock options and the resulting tax advantages; two, software expenses carried as assets rather than write-offs; three, the low salaries associated with stock options; four, certain financial market maneuvers, such as share buy-back programs.

Fourth, not only were no real profits achieved but also no real investments made. Only they could have provided a basis for genuine increases in productivity. The capital stock is still at the same level as it was in the 1960s. The savings rate dropped from about 19 percent at the end of the 1980s to less than zero percent at the end of the 1990s.

Fifth, the stock market boom was never based on genuine value creation but on disinformation by Wall Street and on the exorbitant indebtedness of all sectors of the American economy – most recently at a ratio of 1:3. For each additional dollar of national product, around three additional dollars of debt were needed.

Sixth, the highly praised American budget miracle never happened either. America's public debt is still rising, and has now reached a higher level than ever before. It can be looked up on the internet every day.

The past years' figures on the American economy have been wrong, or have been falsely interpreted and propagated by the media. This has steered people's actions in the wrong direction. The result has been a massive misallocation of resources. Now that the illusion of an eternal boom turns out to be wrong as well, there is a need for major corrections which will take a long time to complete.

I will say this again: It is wrong to believe that American businesses are successful due to superior management and advanced corporate governance. And it is dangerous and naïve to try to copy American ways of thinking and acting in Europe and Asia.

Corporate Success

Few things have been more grossly misjudged by self-proclaimed experts than the so-called New Economy. And few things are as blatantly misunderstood and misused, on a regular basis, as are key financial indicators. In hindsight, the second half of the 1990s will be considered a period of collective erring on key questions of corporate management.

Actually, this was the origin of the systematic misuse of economic resources which later led to the collapse of the financial system and ultimately caused one of the worst economic crises in history.

Before that time, there had hardly been any problems with the definition of corporate success. At least among specialists it was clear how the term was to be understood. Today, "corporate success" is one of the dangerous terms. Balance sheet scandals, compensation excesses, and the general misdirection in business were caused not least by a degenerated concept of corporate success.

Turbulent times require clear, meaningful and fashion-resistant standards. What is a good deal? When is a company healthy? What are reliable indicators of success or failure? The more emphasis is placed on financials, the more important is a broad-based assessment.

There are six key indicators of corporate success. Only if they are known in conjunction and over a longer period of time is it possible to judge the state of a company – but the outcome will then be all the more accurate and reliable. Together, these measures form the management's "cockpit". They are also the key factors of any corporate strategy.

The first indicator is the company's market position in each of its lines of business. Unfortunately there is no single parameter which, in itself, adequately portrays the market position. In most cases people go by market share. But what is that? Is it defined geographically or by customer groups, by sales channels or applications, by direct customers or end users? Are the market shares of substitute products known? What about quality and customer value, brand awareness and image? Every company needs to determine for itself what factors adequately portray its market position, and develop indicators for those factors. The continuous improvement of the overall market position – not just market share – must be the cornerstone of any corporate strategy. If that is the case you can usually not go wrong.

The second indicator is innovation performance. Companies which cease to innovate will almost irreversibly go down the drain. Typical indicators of innovation performance, though by far not the only ones, are time to market, hit versus flop rate, and the share of sales of new products. Internal innovation also belongs under this heading. It includes the ongoing renewal of systems and processes, methods and practices, structures and technologies. Similar to what has been said about market position, every company needs to determine the fields of innovation that are relevant for its line of business, and determine and monitor appropriate indicators. Decreasing innovativeness is a warning signal of the first order. It can be recognized long before its effects become apparent in the tools of the accounting department. Continuous renewal must therefore be a standard component of corporate strategy.

The third area is the company's productivity, or more precisely: its productivities. Years ago it used to be enough to measure one kind of productivity: that of labor. Now we need at least three productivity figures: labor productivity, capital productivity, and productivity over time. And we would be well advised to start thinking about a fourth one: the productivity of knowledge – although so far nobody knows how it should be defined. Productivities are only meaningful if expressed in terms of value added; that is to say, the value added per employee (labor productivity), per monetary unit invested (capital productivity) or per unit of time. Not every company can permanently keep growing, but every company can keep getting better in the sense of getting more productive. There are no discernible limits to date for the increase in productivity.

The fourth indicator of corporate success is attractiveness to good people. What matters is not so much how many employees leave or join the company (i.e., the churn rate), but what kind. When good people "abandon ship" or when the company finds it hard to recruit them, management had better be on alert. The resignation of good people, no matter what their level of hierarchy, has to become a top-priority issue. The exit interviews with these people – because they usually cannot be stopped from leaving – provide those interested with a prime opportunity for learning the most significant truths that can not be learnt any other way. Signs of erosion in this area will not show in the accounting systems, however sophisticated they may be, nor in any other databases or information pools, be it on the internet or on the intranet.

The fifth measure is liquidity. It is an old truth that a company can manage for quite a while without making profits, but never without liquidity. Profit increases at the expense of liquidity are dangerous, for instance, if higher margins can only be obtained by allowing longer periods of payment. Companies in a profit squeeze will usually do the right thing: they will divest low-performing businesses. Companies in a liquidity squeeze, however, will often respond the wrong way. What they really need to do is divest their best businesses, as those are the only ones that can be sold off in good time and at a high enough price.

The sixth indicator is the company's profit requirement, which can rarely be deduced from the profit as such or from any other of the financial figures appearing on the accounts. It is obtained by answering a question, not by doing the math. It is a consequence of the fact that, strictly speaking, there is no such thing as profit. The only thing that exists is costs: the costs of the current business and those required to stay in business. And if we do insist on talking about profit, we must not cling to the notion of maximum profit. The key question must be: what is the minimum profit we need to stay in business tomorrow? That has nothing to do with a minimalist attitude. Rather, what we will find in the majority of cases is that the minimum, according to this definition, is way above the level that most people would accept as maximum.

Value

The term "value" also belongs in the list of words discussed here. Rarely before has a term been used so much and never, except in Marxist theory, have value-related issues been regarded as so central to economic activity. I am referring to value in an economic sense, not as a moral, ethical or artistic concept.

As a result of the intense discussion about value and the frequent use of the word "value", people have almost forgotten that there is no such thing as economic values. All there is are prices.

The value of anything, regardless of what it is, is the price that the next buyer is prepared to pay. The price paid by the last buyer has no significance. The amount a person has paid for an item may determine his own financial situation, and therefore his own ideas, hopes, and negotiating tactics for the next transaction. However, it is insignificant – except as a theoretical concept. The reality is the next transaction and the price paid for it.

The valuation methods used, no matter by what criteria they have been designed, may well provide a basis for negotiation objectives, for wishes, hopes, and the placing of orders on the stock markets. It is also quite possible that, for a while, the value previously calculated actually emerges as the valid price. This can give the impression that valuations have an impact on pricing.

However, on the stock markets we find daily examples of how far removed prices can be from the values stated. Arguments using values, and referring to the overvaluation or undervaluation of shares, for example, are therefore pointless. Let me repeat: There is no value but the price that the next buyer pays.

This is why it is essentially wrong to talk about company internal value chains, a concept first introduced by Michael Porter.[15] There are no values insight a company, only costs. Only outside the company can costs be converted into something of value – namely, when a customer settles an invoice or pays a price.

Thinking in terms of values holds another, possibly more serious danger. It influences marketing in a dangerous way. It leads us back to the notion that the effort and expense involved in producing a product determine its value and therefore its price. In other words, it appears to legitimize cost-driven pricing. The reality in the markets, however, is exactly the opposite – what we see there is price-driven costing.

Any company that calculates the price of a product by starting with its own costs and adding extra charges for risk and profit is likely to maneuver itself out of the market. Instead, the starting point should be the existing market price, from which a reasonable profit should be deducted; everything else from development to sales must be covered by what remains. This is the only way to avoid operating in disregard of the realities of the market.

This is a fact which particularly the New Economy firms, who believed they had invented new laws of doing business, failed to understand. Even today, software firms often point to the expense and effort that went into the development of a program. Then they go on to talk about the value of the knowledge comprised in the product, thinking that this suffices to justify they price they are asking.

Under the logic of the market economy, this way of thinking is wrong in terms of the logic of the market economy, and therefore it is dangerous. And if anyone is not convinced by that logic, a look at India and its software developers should provide enough evidence: the only economic reality is price.

The lesson to be learnt from the current financial and economic crisis is clear. At the beginning of 2008, the stock of the U.S. investment bank Bear Sterns was quoted at almost 180 dollars. Then in March, long before the actual outbreak of the crisis, it was at approximately 2 dollars – and shortly after that the bank went broke. The exaggerated quotes had hit price bottom – which in this case equaled zero because there were no more buyers. The margins in between had been mere illusions.

Sustainability

As the realization spreads that many of the terms lately used by the financial scene are actually misleading, the word "sustainability" is gaining popularity. It is a step forward because the word invokes notions of longevity, durability, and continuity. It is the opposite of short-term behavior aimed at making quick profits.

Still, the term has its dangerous sides, or at least its downsides. Since it is used more and more frequently and threatens to become fashionable, I want to take this opportunity to point out its risks.

The term is most frequently found in the environmental context, where it is associated with careful use of resources or, in general, with the ability to maintain a condition, a behavior, or a way of doing business over the long term. The dominant notion is stability.

As important as this may be – companies and most other societal institutions must be capable of more. They must be able to keep adapting themselves to completely unforeseen developments, to situations and events that no one predicted because they were not predictable.

When we refer to sustainability in cybernetics, we speak of stability in the sense already mentioned. However, what is needed is the ability to keep creating new stable situations – qualitites known as ultra-stability and polystability.

As I have said before, sustainability represents a major step forward. The logical next step must be viability.

Viability is the ability to maintain the capacity to function over an unlimited period. One illustration of the concept is this: when a resource has been used up, a system must be able to switch to another resource. It must prepare itself in good time and make the necessary adjustments to allow for the changeover to the new resource. The same thing applies to a move from one technology to another one that substitutes it, from one production method to a newer and better one, and from one sales channel to a new, more lucrative and more up-to-date channel. It is the ability to evolve.

There is a sophisticated theory of viability that originated in management cybernetics, as well as a model based on it: the Viable System Model. Both were developed by the management cyberneticist Stafford Beer, who sadly died in August 2002.[11]

Globalization

The word "globalization" and everything to do with it need to be included in the list of dangerous words. The risk associated with these terms is that they induce managers to adopt wrong theories and, as a result, false strategies and wrong measures. Pressure from outside often plays a part in this: the view taken by the media, the thinking of shareholders, and zeitgeist in general.

The word "globalization" is so widely used that we are led to believe it is clear and unambiguous. It is not. "Globalization" has many meanings and anyone can bustle around with it in any way they please.

People in any company will therefore be well advised to carefully think about how they wish to use the word. Even the far less pretentious term "internationalization" is anything but clear. Exactly in how many countries does a company have to carry on what percentage of its business activities to be able to call itself "international"? There are no criteria for this. Anyone with a mailbox in the Bahamas can call himself "international". Similar applies to the word "multinational": it also has little real meaning, except that it is often used as a term of abuse for the giant groups.

Peter F. Drucker has been using the term "transnational" since the mid-1990s when referring to things unrelated to the nation state or to national consciousness. There are only two things he considers transnational: money and information.

Globalization does not imply that the whole world is turning into a "village", as romantics and futurologists are fond of saying. The prerequisites for that are completely lacking. How should we imagine a village populated by over six billion people? They will never form a village, even if we put the word in quotation marks. Anyone who has visited some of the world's biggest cities will be aware of that. One cannot help wondering at the innumerable zeitgeist authors rambling on about the global village, grandiloquently but clearly devoid of insight.

Globalization does not mean that the cultures of the world will have to grow closer together, and agree to be guided by the Western way of life and thinking – which, by the way, is by no means uniform in itself. It is much more likely that existing differences will be accentuated further.

Nor does globalization mean that every company or its products have to be represented in every country around the world. Even among the biggest companies there are precious few whose products are almost ubiquitous; Coca Cola is probably one of them. Most companies continue to be selective in where they do business, and for good reasons.

For the time being, globalization, in my opinion, means three things:

First – that no place on earth can be ruled out entirely as a venue for the various aspects of business activity. This means that on principle, any stage of the business process, from development through sourcing and on to sales, can be located anywhere in the world.

Second – that national frontiers can no longer effectively protect against competition. Nontheless, a revival of protectionism cannot be ruled out – indeed, it is something I consider very likely to happen. The American steel industry is a prime example of what regulators will fall back on as a last resort, swiftly and without the slightest qualm: protective tariffs. Nevertheless, it is getting increasingly difficult to effectively shelter domestic suppliers from competition.

Third – that it is important to monitor global developments in order to avoid being surprised. That does not mean, however, that it is necessary to *act* globally.

The third aspect, in my view, is the most important one for the vast majority of companies. Even in the distant future, by far not every company will have to operate globally. There will, however, be more and more, including small and medium-sized firms, which will need to monitor the global landscape: it is the only way they can avoid being taken unawares by competitors, or surprised by new developments they had failed to notice – in particular with regard to sourcing and manufacturing opportunities. This in itself is difficult enough and quite expensive.

For entrepreneurs affected by my first point above, it is sometimes worthwhile looking back in history – especially when the supposed uniqueness and unprecedentedness of today's globalization trends are propounded all too insistently. In the 15th or 16th century, the merchants of Upper Italy did not need to be told that there was a whole world out there. The Venetians and Florentines of the Renaissance did deals that spanned the entire known world. The German Fuggers learned from them and for about 200 years operated a global organization. They had their "factors" (a contemporaneous term for executive managers) in all the important countries and cities of the world, they did business with all of Europe, they dominated half of South America – mind you, without the benefit of mobile phones, fax machines, e-mails, or jet planes – and were economic survivors of the spectacular bankruptcies of the crowned heads of the House of Habsburg.

The Jesuit order operated all over the world as a global trading and knowledge organization, in Japan and China, in India and in South America. So successful were the Jesuits that they were considered dangerous, which is why the order was prohibited in several countries.

Globalization is older than satellite television and the internet. It has had its times of splendor and its setbacks. Perhaps the most important thing that managers can learn from its history is … to maintain a sense of proportion.

Profit

After centuries of the word "profit" being used – initially by merchants, then by scientists, and finally by consultants, auditors and investment bankers – one should think that its meaning has been defined beyond doubt. It has not.

As a result of the boom and bubble economy, we now know – perhaps better than ever – how to generate and manipulate profit expectations, juggle with profit figures, and mislead the media. Yet the term "profit" still is not really understood, which is why it is used incorrectly and often improperly.

The more a manager talks about profit, the more skepticism is in order, and the more important it is to find out what he really means, particularly when he refers to optimum or maximum profit.

For the purposes of managing a company, the concept of maximum profit is actually useless. What is much more helpful is its opposite – minimum profit – which refers to how much a company needs to earn in order to stay in business. This is a question entirely different from the issues dealt with in accounting. It cannot even be answered with accounting methods.

For the truly professional management of a company, I suggest going yet another step further and ceasing to refer to profit altogether. After all, in the final analysis there are no profits, only costs. There are two kinds: those of the existing business and those required for staying in business.

The former kind is well known to us, as these costs can be carried in the books. Those of the latter category are unknown – they cannot be entered in the books because we do not have documentary evidence of them. Nevertheless, they are just as real as the costs that can be entered. If we cannot raise the money for the second type of costs the company will not have a future. As long as the term "costs" is used, major management errors are hardly possible – but too narrow a definition of profit has always been a major step toward a company's ruin.

Interest Rate Cuts

Why should companies which were highly indebted even before the crisis and are therefore under repayment pressure enter additional liabilities during the crisis? No matter how low interest rates are, a responsible entrepreneur will not do this, for it is enough of a struggle to settle the existing debts.

Doing Business Is Hardly a Matter of Interest Rates

In the real world, businesses do not focus on interest rates but on the opportunities in their markets. If they are good, interest rates do not matter so much. If they are bad, even the lowest interest rates will be too high to make an investment.

For investment decisions in the real economy, financing costs are far from having the significance they are theoretically assumed to have. But as most economists have little experience with real-life businesses and business management, they are unfamiliar with the typical entrepreneurial mindset. This is why they usually assume that entrepreneurs are out to maximize their profits. Cases like this do exist, of course, but in entrepreneurial reality there are very different situations and goals, such as the goal to stay solvent and avoid running into more debt.

Change in Interest Rates More Important Than Absolute Levels

In entrepreneurial real life, one factor which matters much more than the absolute level of interest rates is how they change. That is why central banks ought not to reduce rates but actually to increase them, if they really wish to produce a boost effect on investment activities.

Certain, but by no means all investments might be brought forward if business leaders had to expect interest rates increases: in that case, investments would be cheaper to finance today than tomorrow.

The opposite is true for a downward interest rate trend. It causes people to sit tight as interest rates are expected to be lower tomorrow. So any investments that can be deferred will be. The result is so-called attentism – a reluctant 'wait and see' attitude that has a kind of freezing effect on the economy.

In short, the central banks and governments with all their well-intended actions are actually exacerbating the crisis.

Doing Business

The main purpose of work is often ignored, sometimes even unknown. As a consequence, the true nature of doing business is not really understood, either. This is extremely dangerous once drastic reforms become necessary which affect the perceived vested rights of the welfare society.

Why does man work? Why is there such a thing as business? Why is it done in a certain way?

Work and economic activity in general are commonly explained with certain forms of human striving and wanting: Man – so we hear – wishes to satisfy certain needs. As a consumer, man strives for benefit or the fulfillment of his needs. As entrepreneur, man wishes to achieve profit, or growth, or both. As employee, man works because he has been motivated. As manager, he feels called upon to be innovative.

Obviously, then, a set of psychological elements must be considered the drivers of economic activity. Not only does it sound plausible, it is largely established theory. But is it really true? Do the subjective elements of wanting, wishing, and striving account for the pressures in the business sector? Why do people face up to that pressure instead of evading or ignoring it? The answers: because of the competition. But is that really the whole truth?

This common perception of doing business overlooks the most important point by far: people do not work and companies do not do business because they wish to but because they have to. They are forced to.

Where does this constraint come from? It follows from the simple but undeniable fact that people and companies have assumed *obligations* which have been specified with regard to scope and time, and which they must fulfill. Or, put in simpler terms: They have liabilities.

A part of the underlying debt agreements has been concluded voluntarily and could have been prevented. The respective acts of purchase, such as installment, leasing, or credit card purchases, could have been postponed. However, once a debt agreement has been concluded it takes its inexorable and irreversible effect: It constitutes a duty of performance – not only to the extent of the obligation itself but also including interest. Establishing obligations may be voluntary – their settlement is not.

That alone, however, does not suffice to understand the dynamics of business. By far the larger part of debt contracts are concluded involuntarily. All productions and all the work need to be financed in advance. Only after something has been produced will there be buyers for it, and salaries only after the work has been done. Pre-financing leads to compulsory debt contracts and to additional costs in the form of interest rates.

No matter what the debtor's aim, intention, or motivation – he is forced to generate not only the loan itself, delivering an output which he otherwise might not have delivered. (In the absence of that obligation, he would have been able to take time out, and with a perfectly good conscience.) In addition, however, the debtor is forced to deliver in excess of that output, to the extent that the interest incurred can be covered.

There is little talk about this cause of economic activity, the typical rush and pressure – which is remarkable, in particular as we currently have the highest debt, both in absolute and relative terms, that ever existed worldwide. The current low interest rates make it easier to bear than it would be with high interest rates. Still, the obligation to supererogation is astronomical in absolute terms. This cause of economic activity is totally independent of psychological motives and other aims, wishes or intentions.

The sum of all contractual obligations, multiplied with the respective interest rate, equals the sum of the minimum economic supererogation required to prevent economic ruin. We owe this insight to one of the best economists I know: Paul C. Martin[16]. Based on the papers by Gunnar Heinsohn and Otto Steiger[17], he has played an essential role in developing what we refer to as debitist economic theory. Anyone unfamiliar with that theory will be unable to truly understand economics.

We are used to putting people in categories: consumers and manufacturers, employees and employers, suppliers and demanders. While these categories do have significance, they offer relatively little in the way of explanation. Categories with much more significance are those of debtors and creditors.

From this debitist view, the market is more than a meeting place for supply and demand: first and foremost, it is the place where indebted manufacturers attempt to raise the funds required to cover their debt. Capitalism is not a system designed to promote the maximization of profits. It may appear to be so from a contemplative perspective – one that is far removed from economic reality. In capitalism, it does not matter at all whether or not someone makes a profit. Capitalism is a system where bills have to be paid. That is the only useful definition. At bottom, what matters is liquidity, not profit. The bill is paid by the debtor – as long as he is able to pay it. Once that is no longer the case, the creditor will pay instead, by writing off the bad debt.

In economies undergoing a recession or crisis, these dynamics become apparent in a gloomy way – in Japan, in parts of South-East Asia, in Argentina – but also everywhere else, because an increasing part of the population of all countries is slipping into the debt trap.

Neither people's demands nor the perpetually discussed psychological elements (as important as they may be) are crucial to a true understanding of economic activity. People can always lower their standards in everyday life – if only there were no bill collectors.

Plunging stock prices and property values would not be a problem to anyone, if they had been paid in cash and not on credit. Hence, economic recovery does not start in people's heads, as naïve advertising slogans proclaim. It begins and ends with debts.

Rationality

Economists and politicians often complain about a presumed lack of rationality when consumers and entrepreneurs do not act the way they should, according to economic theory. Among other things, the experts feel that the so-called "economic subjects" do not make enough of an effort to master the crisis, despite a massive injection of funds and low interest rates. Consumers consume too little, entrepreneurs postpone their investments. Some experts even speak of "irrationality", indirectly accusing people of behaving in ways that are detrimental to the economy.

Human behavior only seems irrational, however, when judged from the one-dimensional viewpoint of pure economics. This viewpoint exists in academia but not in reality. In real life we have a multi-dimensional society where doing business is one of many important things; but it is by far not the only thing on people's minds.

From a holistic standpoint, business leaders behave highly rationally when, for instance, they do not make investments in spite of low interest rates, simply because business prospects are poor. That this kind of behavior does not fit with economic theory may well be a fault of the theory, not of the entrepreneurs.

By the same token, consumers' seemingly irrational behavior becomes easier to understand if one takes into account that they are human beings and not only consumers. In times of crisis, people have other goals besides consumption. Instead of consuming, they find it to be more sensible to save their money. They accumulate reserves for a future that is uncertain, for a possible loss of employment, for sickness, old age, education of their offspring, provisions for future care needs of elderly parents, and many other risks.

Their actions are driven by what they need to do today, as they cannot tell what things will be like tomorrow. This can hardly be called irrational; on the contrary, it is perhaps the most rational question to be asked when one has to act under the condition of an irremediable lack of information.

Another point to consider is that today's consumption is very different from what it used to be some twenty or thirty years ago, or in general at the time when the great economic concepts emerged. At least in developed countries and for an increasing number of people, the primary purpose of consumption is no longer to cover urgent needs. To most, consumption is much more about satisfying desires. This, however, is something they can do without, if need be, particularly when they are hardly missing anything even when they forgo certain purchases.

For many people, consumption has reached an unprecedeted level of saturation. For the first time in world history, there is the possibility of forgoing things without experiencing want or deprivation. For instance, the consumption of many consumer goods can be drastically reduced before people will feel they lack something. It is even more obvious with durable consumer goods. For instance, most people could drive their cars several years longer without actually missing anything essential.

For all these reasons, economic policies to stimulate consumption are not very likely to be effective – not because people are not irrational but, on the contrary, because of their pronounced rationality.

Notes

1 We owe it to Linda Pelzmann that mass psychology has been integrated into economic science. Economists, psychologists, sociologists, information scientists, managers, and students are no longer flustered when asked to explain irrational behaviors in the capital markets occuring in boom and panic phases.

2 Depending on the source, we usually find something along the lines of "extraordinary power, divine favor or gift" when the religious meaning of charisma is referred to; according to the *Meyers* encyclopedia (in German), the sociological meaning of the word is a characteristic talent for a certain service, in particular for taking on a leadership role and, related to it, for an irrational domination over others (*Meyers Großes Handlexikon; Brockhaus multimedial* 2001).

3 In what follows, I use the terms "emotion" and "feeling" as synonymous with one another. In the specialist literature certain distinctions are made between the two but these are of no significance for the present purpose.

4 Among the most interesting studies in this field are those presented by Dietrich Dörner and his colleagues, such as the Tanaland and Lohhausen experiments. For an overview see "The Logic of Failure", 1996.

5 Hayek, Friedrich August von: Law, Legislation and Liberty, Vol. 3, London 1979, 155ff.

6 Among others, see Eccles, John: *Evolution of the Brain; Creation of the Self*, New York, 1989 (reprint 1991).

7 Roth, G. in: *Süddeutsche Zeitung* [German daily newspaper], issue of April 11, 2000.

8 Definition according to the German *Duden* dictionary. The psychological meaning of the term, as given here, must be clearly distinguished from identification in the sense of determining the identity of, for example, a person (as done for instance by the police) or the identity of a thing (such as a work of art or a stolen car).

9 Historical or contemporary indications sometimes point to the particular performance, for instance, of indoctrinated combat units under totalitarian systems. I find them unconvincing. The units achieved temporary but no lasting successes. Apart from that, the ethical acceptability of such leadership (management) methods would have to be questioned.

10 See also the numerous books by Viktor Frankl, such as *Man's Search for Ultimate Meaning*, New York, 2000.

11 See Beer, Stafford: *Brain of the Firm*, London 1972, 2nd edition, London 1994, and: *The Heart of Enterprise*, London, 2nd edition, 1984, as well as the website of the Cwarel Isaf Institute www.managementkybernetik.com.

12 Drucker, Peter F.: *Managing for Results*, London 1964.

13 I am aware that there was such a thing as workshop painting; however, it was not causal to the development of the great art of painting and the creative works of art, although I do not deny that teams can be creative, too.

14 On this subject, see Drucker, Peter F.: *Management: Tasks, Responsibilities, Practices,* London 1973.

15 Porter, Michael E.: *Competitive Advantage*, New York 1985

16 Martin, Paul C./Lüftl, Walter: *Der Kapitalismus. Ein System, das funktioniert* ["Capitalism. A System That Works"], Berlin 1990.

17 Heinsohn, Gunnar/Steiger, Otto: *Eigentum, Zins und Geld. Ungelöste Rätsel der Wirtschaftswissenschaft,* ["Property, Interest and Money. Unsolved Puzzles in Economics"] Reinbek near Hamburg, 2002.

18 Drucker, Peter F.: *The Age of Discontinuity. Guidelines to Our Changing Society*, London 1969, Neuauflage 1992.

19 Beer, Stafford: *Beyond Dispute. The Invention of Team Syntegrity*, Chichester 1993.

References

Beer, Stafford: *Brain of the Firm*, London 1972, 2nd edition, 1994.

Beer, Stafford: *The Heart of Enterprise*, London, 1984 and 1994, and Website of the Cwarel Isaf Institutes www.managementkybernetik.com.

Beer, Stafford: *Beyond Dispute. The Invention of Team Syntegrity*, Chichester, 1993.

Dörner, Dietrich: *Die Logik des Misslingens. Strategisches Denken in komplexen Situationen*, 5th edition, Reinbek near Hamburg, 2003.

Drucker, Peter F.: *Managing for Results*, London, 1964.

Drucker, Peter F.: *Management: Tasks, Responsibilities, Practices*, London, 1973.

Drucker, Peter F.: *The Age of Discontinuity*, London 1969; Neuauflage 1992.

Eccles, John: *Die Evolution des Gehirns, die Erschaffung des Selbst*, 3rd edition, Munich, 2002. [English Edition: *Evolution of the Brain; Creation of the Self*, New York, 1989]

Frankl, Viktor: *Man's Search for Ultimate Meaning* , New York, 2000.

Hayek, Friedrich A.: *Law, Legislation and Liberty*, Vol. 3, London, 1979.

Häusel, Hans-Georg: *Think Limbic! Die Macht des Unbewussten verstehen und nutzen für Motivation, Marketing, Management*, Planegg near Munich, 2003, 4th edition 2005.

Heinsohn, Gunnar: *Privateigentum, Patriarchat, Geldwirtschaft. Eine sozialtheoretische Rekonstruktion zur Antike*, Frankfurt am Main, 1984.

Heinsohn, Gunnar/Steiger, Otto: *Eigentum, Zins und Geld. Ungelöste Rätsel der Wirtschaftswissenschaft*, Marburg, 1996, 2nd edition, 2002.

Heinsohn, Gunnar/Steiger, Otto: *Eigentumsökonomik. Eigentumstheorie des Wirtschaftens versus Wirtschaftstheorie ohne Eigentum. Ergänzungsband zur Neuauflage „Eigentum, Zins und Geld"*, Marburg, 2002.

Malik, Fredmund: *Die richtige Corporate Governance. Mit wirksamer Unternehmensaufsicht Komplexität meistern.* Frankfurt am Main, 2008. (English translation expected for 2011).

Malik, Fredmund: *Managing, Performing, Living. Effective Management For a New Era*, New York, 2003.

Martin, Paul C./Lüftl, Walter: *Der Kapitalismus. Ein System, das funktioniert*, Berlin, 1990.

Pelzmann, Linda: *Triumph der Massenpsychologie. Rahmenbedingungen und Regeln*. In: m.o.m.®Malik on Management-Letter, Vol. 10, 11/2002, 184–200.

Pelzmann, Linda: *Kollektive Panik*. In: m.o.m.®Malik on Management-Letter, Vol. 10, 02/2003, 20–33.

Porter, Michael E.: *Competitive Advantage*, New York, 1985.